EDMUND MORRIS "KYAIYII" 1871 - 1913

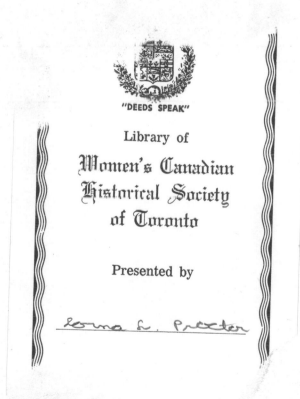

EDMUND MORRIS "KYAIYII" 1871 - 1913

by

Geoffrey Simmins
Michael Parke-Taylor

organized by the
Norman Mackenzie Art Gallery
University of Regina
Regina, Saskatchewan

1984

EDMUND MORRIS "KYAIYII" 1871 - 1913

20 January - 26 February 1984

ISBN 0-920922-23-6

Copyright © 1984 Norman Mackenzie Art Gallery

Designed and published by the Norman Mackenzie Art Gallery, University of Regina, Regina, Saskatchewan, Canada S4S 0A2.

The exhibition and catalogue have been made possible by National Museums of Canada, Museums Assistance Program.

Printed by Merit Printing Company, Regina

Front Cover: Edmund Morris, *Moses,* 1910
           Collection of the Government of Saskatchewan, Regina (cat. 28)

Frontispiece: *Edmund Montague Morris*
           Manitoba Archives, Winnipeg

CONTENTS

FOREWORD

Edmund Morris was proud of his honorary Indian name, "Kyaiyii", Bear Robe. Along with this, he treasured other shared romantic notions about trekking west and recording forever a way of life and a generation of Indian leaders that was quickly disappearing. They did disappear along with the remains of nineteenth-century Canada still colliding with the twentieth, when Morris came West. Their influence and memory have not disappeared, however, living on in the traditions of their descendants and commemorated in images by artists such as Edmund Morris. His interest in painting his subjects was not limited to memento; his real intention was immortalization of his subjects as works of art.

Unfortunately, much of the art made by Edmund Morris along with that made by the native culture he so admired has been sequestered in museum ethnology departments. This practice has slowed their analysis as works of art. Michael Parke-Taylor and Geoffrey Simmins are to be congratulated upon recognizing the merit of these works and thereby producing a superb exhibition and a thorough catalogue; the first to establish Edmund Morris in a Canadian art historical context.

As usual, it is the prompting of the Mackenzie permanent collection which has suggested a research exhibition of such scale. In this case, along with our pastel drawing, *Chief Star Blanket,* the familiar yet overlooked drawings which have hung for many years in the rotunda of the Saskatchewan Legislative Building are the focus of the exhibition. Michael Parke-Taylor has set out the story of the Saskatchewan Portrait Commission in his catalogue essay, while guest curator Geoffrey Simmins describes Morris' full career. The Mackenzie Art Gallery is grateful to the Government of Saskatchewan, as well as to the other public and private collectors who have lent fragile works to an important exhibition.

The problem of conserving pastel drawings is well known in the art museum. The chalk pigments are easily moved if the drawing is jarred. Yet, works of art must be seen, analysed, documented and appreciated as part of society's process of cultural identification. Curators and conservators are constantly faced with difficult decisions — to show a fragile piece and risk some deterioration or preserve it in safety, but unseen. The legacy of Edmund Morris is victim to this problem. The richness and depth of a pastel drawing can never be reproduced. It is a great privilege to see these works in exhibition.

The Exhibition Assistance Programme, Museums Assistance Programme of the National Museums of Canada Corporation has been most generous in funding this exhibition.

Carol A. Phillips
Director

4

ACKNOWLEDGEMENTS

The curators acknowledge gratefully the assistance and support of many individuals and institutions. Dennis Reid, Curator of Canadian Historical Art at the Art Gallery of Ontario in Toronto helped locate paintings by Morris and offered a sympathetic sounding board for ideas on the artist. Mary Fitz-Gibbon, research assistant, Royal Ontario Museum generously shared her transcription of Morris' diaries and her great enthusiasm for the artist. Others to whom thanks are due include Joan Murray, Director, The Robert McLaughlin Gallery, Oshawa; Fern Bayer, Curator of the Government of Ontario Art Collection, Toronto; Ken McCarthy, Curator of Fine and Decorative Arts, Provincial Museum of Alberta, Edmonton; Charles Hill, Curator of Canadian Art, National Gallery of Canada, Ottawa; Delia Laird, Artwork Supervisor, Government of Saskatchewan, Regina; Hunter Bishop, Archivist, Arts and Letters Club, Toronto; Elizabeth Blight, Head of Stills Division, Provincial Archives of Manitoba, Winnipeg; Rebecca Sisler; Ms. Jean McGill; Judy Hall, Canadian Ethnology Service, National Museum of Man, Ottawa; Ken Lister, Ethnology Department, Royal Ontario Museum, Toronto; Andrew Oko, Curator, Art Gallery of Hamilton; Patricia Ainslie, Curator of Collections, Glenbow Museum, Calgary; Lorna Procter, Archivist, Women's Canadian Historical Society, Toronto; David Kotin, Metropolitan Toronto Library, Toronto; Ray Christenson and his staff, Photographic Services, Government of Saskatchewan, Regina; Don Hall, AV Services, University of Regina; Mr. Harold Groves, King City, Ontario; and the other private collectors who graciously lent works to the exhibition

We are particularly grateful for the forebearance of Larry Pfaff and the staff of the Reference Library of the Art Gallery of Ontario; and of Alan Suddon and the staff of the Fine Art Department of the Metropolitan Toronto Library Board. We also thank the staff of the Ontario Archives, Toronto; Queen's University Archives, Kingston; The Public Archives of Canada, Ottawa; The Provincial Archives of Manitoba, Winnipeg; and the Saskatchewan Archives, Regina.

G.S.   M.P-T.

LENDERS TO THE EXHIBITION

The Art Gallery of Hamilton
The Art Gallery of Ontario, Toronto
Glenbow Museum, Calgary
The Government of Alberta, Edmonton
The Government of Ontario, Toronto
The Government of Saskatchewan, Regina
Metropolitan Toronto Library
National Gallery of Canada, Ottawa
Norman Mackenzie Art Gallery, Regina
Provincial Archives of Manitoba, Winnipeg
Royal Ontario Museum, Canadiana Collection, Toronto
Women's Canadian Historical Society, Toronto
Harold Groves, King City
Joan and W. Ross Murray, Whitby
C. R. Osler, Toronto
William K. Schwarz and Nancy Schwarz, Cambridge

ABBREVIATIONS

AGO Art Gallery of Ontario (formerly the Art Gallery of Toronto)

AGH Art Gallery of Hamilton

CAC Canadian Art Club

CNE Canadian National Exhibition, Toronto (formerly the Toronto Industrial Exhibition)

NGC National Gallery of Canada, Ottawa

OCA Ontario College of Art, Toronto

OSA Ontario Society of Artists

RCA Royal Canadian Academy

ROM Royal Ontario Museum

Edmund Morris, *Chief Star Blanket,* 1910
Norman Mackenzie Art Gallery, Regina
(cat. 26)

INTRODUCTION

On a mid-August day in 1913, while sketching from a railway bridge beside the lower St. Lawrence River near Port Neuf, Quebec, Toronto artist Edmund Morris slipped from the bridge and drowned. Then well-known as an Indian portraitist, landscape painter and dynamic organizer in Canadian art circles, Morris has since his death slipped from memory; today few but specialists remember him. This exhibition, the first major showing of his work since 1928, brings together a representative survey of Morris' considerable if largely unknown output, ranging from large landscapes and Indian portraits to previously unexhibited early drawings and tiny oil sketches. It is the first step in reevaluating his contribution to Canadian art.

Morris' reputation as an artist rests largely on his Indian portraits which have long been recognized for their sympathetic attitude to each sitter and their accurate depiction of native costume. They preserve a valuable record of the last generation of Canadian Indians who could remember life before the white man. These portraits are well represented in the exhibition. The exhibition also provides an opportunity to reexamine Morris' landscapes. Although regarded by many of his contemporaries with less favor than the portraits, the best Morris landscapes have a compelling force and depth of vision that makes them equally memorable. A work such as *Cap Tourmente* for instance (NGC, cat. 12), painted c. 1903, features a cool silvery atmosphere contrasted against the rich brown tones of the landscape. Morris' juicy blobs of pigment and bravura brushwork impart to the painting a dramatic quality reflecting the elemental force of nature. Its loose handling marks it as among the most advanced landscape paintings executed during these years by any Canadian artist.

Morris worked during a transitional period in Canada, when the country was actively striving toward nationhood yet was unsure how to achieve it. Many Canadians today remember the 1890s, the decade when Morris started to paint, as the time when then-Prime Minister Sir Wilfred Laurier optimistically claimed that the twentieth century would be Canada's. It is a significant coincidence that the years bracketed by Morris' career — his return in 1896 from study abroad to his unexpected death in 1913 — coincide almost exactly with Laurier's tenure as prime minister. During these years, Laurier pursued an aggressive expansionist policy that opened up the Canadian West. In quick succession, Saskatchewan, Alberta and Manitoba were carved out of the amorphous 'north-western lands'. Partially as a result of this policy, Canada became a nation in fact as well as in name. Then, after parachuting into World War I as a colony, it emerged from the trenches as a nation in spirit.

The nationalist sentiment accompanying Canada's sudden spurt of growth naturally affected artists. Rumblings among artists about the desirability of developing a national school of painting had been in the air at least since 1894, when Ontario artist W. A. Sherwood wrote an essay with the provocative title, "A National Spirit in Art." Yet it is a peculiar feature of this generation of artists that no one agreed as to what *constituted* a national school of painting, although everyone paid lip service to the concept. Did it mean national subject matter, national style, or simply paintings of any subject or style produced by Canadians? This lack of consensus concerning the attributes of a national school was, in essence, the dilemma faced by Edmund Morris. He produced paintings couched in the styles of Europe yet proudly considered himself a Canadian nationalist. It is part of the puzzle of analyzing Morris' work to reconcile his European technique with his nationalist leanings and subject matter.

Morris would not have asked himself these questions. He painted the country as he saw it and probably gave little thought as to whether his style was Canadian. His nationalism was expressed through his actions. From 1896 to 1910 he crisscrossed the country, making summer trips from his Toronto base to Quebec, northern Ontario and western Canada, often working in the field under arduous conditions to record the changing face of the nation.

Winters were spent in Toronto where he immersed himself in the artistic life of the city. He was a founding member and guiding spirit of the Canadian Art Club, an invitational exhibiting society he felt would demonstrate to the world the high achievement of Canadian painting. His feisty nationalism made him campaign vigorously for the choice of local artists to decorate major public commissions. He was an avid amateur historian, amassing a considerable body of information about his peers; he also wrote a book on early Canadian artists. Yet he has never received his just due in Canadian art history, either for his own painting or for his activities as an organizer, writer and historian. His slip from memory has been almost complete.

One factor helps explain the rapid effacement of his reputation: the change of spirit which accompanied Canada's growth to nationhood. Artists of Morris' generation — which include such prominent painters as James Wilson Morrice and Maurice Cullen — trained in New York and Paris, painted with a palette influenced by stylistic trends developed in these international centres and exhibited their work abroad at least as often as in Canada. Morris, no less than any other Canadian artist of his generation, aspired to recognition from his international peers and painted as they did. Morris shared a basic tenet with these artists: that painting was a gentlemanly pursuit whose values were preserved by academic training. The period may be termed loosely the Era of Canadian Internationalists. Its heyday overlaps by several years on either end the reign of Edward VII, from 1901 to 1910.

No trace of this Edwardian world survived the War, nor did any trace of the easy internationalism of the artists of Morris' generation carry through to post-war Canada. A new, narrowly-defined and aggressive nationalism reared its head, in art no less than in politics. Painting seemed to call for a new stylistic expression, divorced from the past and freed from the academies. After all, many artists may have reasoned, what had Europe brought — or wrought — except the same old internecine squabbles among its inbred leaders? Artists such as Morris, manifestly part of the old school of Internationalists, were shrugged off by the new breed of Canadian artists as an embarrassment, almost a colonial precursor of responsible government as it were. Morris' painting was dismissed out of hand, mostly on stylistic grounds. His darkly-hued paintings, with their emphasis on subtle, moody transitions, were aeons away from the art of the new generation, epitomized by the Group of Seven. These painters thought themselves raw, sharp and elemental, like a newly splintered rock from the

Canadian Shield. By the time the Group held its first collective exhibition at the Art Gallery of Toronto in May, 1920, the chasm which split their art from Morris' was as immense as the vast political gulf which split Canada before and after the war. A new spirit had been sounded — and when it was, Morris' art was found to be irrevocably out of step with the times.

We are now distant from those once intensely-felt concerns; the noisy nationalism attending the rise of the Group has been superseded by a greater maturity. We may now hope to wear the mantle of our nationalism with an easier hand gripping it around us. An artist such as Morris, whose gloomy, tenebrous paintings still have the power to move and charm us, deserves to be reinterpreted as part of the process of bridging the gaps in our knowledge of Canadian painting leading to the emergence of the Group of Seven.

Geoffrey Simmins

Edmund Montague Morris was born in Perth, Ontario, 18 December 1871 into a family with a distinguished record of public service:[1] His grandfather was the Hon. William Morris, member of the Legislative Assembly of Upper Canada from 1820 to 1836; his father was the Hon. Alexander Morris, who held a seat in the Federal Parliament from 1861 to 1872. From 1869 to 1872 Morris' father was Minister of Inland Revenue in Sir John A. Macdonald's government. Ill health forced him to resign his seat in 1872, and Macdonald appointed him that year Chief Justice for the Court of Queen's Bench in Manitoba. That same year, however, despite Morris' frail health, Macdonald appointed him Lieutenant-Governor of Manitoba and the Northwest Territories, a position he held until 1877. He proved an able and fair administrator and was responsible for hammering out land settlement treaties with the Indians under his jurisdiction. Many of the Indians still remembered him with respect when Edmund went among them to paint some years later.

Edmund passed his earliest years in Fort Garry (now Winnipeg), surrounded by open prairie, Indians and government officials. His earliest drawings (not in the exhibition) are of the fort itself, events in which his father had played some role, and views of important local residences such as Lord Strathcona's.[2] Although artistically undistinguished and laborious in technique, these drawings evince his early interest in historical subjects, harbingers of his mature interests.

After returning to Ontario in 1877, where Morris' father served in the provincial legislature from 1878 to 1886, the family summered on Lake Joseph, in fashionable Muskoka. It must have been a happy time for Edmund, who spent his time canoeing, boating and sailing. In an 1886 diary entry, he writes, "to Muskoka again in our new house which was built early in the spring. A long walk leads up to it amongst rock and Norway pine. It has a broad verandah on three sides and one above. (And you hear the lap of the waves and the moan of the pine. The air is perfect.)"[3] Government officials and Indians still came to see his father; in 1886, for instance, Edmund records in his diary, "Col. Macdonald and four Cree chiefs on their way to interview Sir John [Macdonald] stopped off to see father."[4] Such experiences made Edmund aware of the rapidly-vanishing world of the Indian; this awareness, coupled with a strong sense of the positive values of the Canadian landscape engendered by his early years spent on the Prairies and in small-town Ontario, were cornerstones in his development as an artist.

Edmund decided quite early in his life to become an artist. His father at first put up mild resistance, steering Edmund toward architecture. In an 1888 diary entry, Edmund writes, "Although I had often thought of going right in for art, it was thought better that I should try architecture."[5] A short stint with prominent Toronto architect and family friend Frank Darling was not a success, however, and in another diary entry, in January 1889, Edmund writes, "Architecture is uncongenial to me. Lengthy calculations are not my line .... After six months I abandoned the idea of going in for it."[6] Thereafter his father gave in, and that autumn Edmund entered the Toronto studio of William Cruikshank, whose standing among artists was as high as

Darling's was in architecture. Edmund's father died that year shortly after suffering a stroke while at Muskoka.

Morris applied himself assiduously in 1889, attending Cruikshank's regular classes and sketching nights at the Art Students League in Toronto. After a year with Cruikshank, he left for New York, where he studied at the Art Students League there under Kenyon Cox, William Chase, Henry Siddons Mowbray and George de Forest Brush.[7] This New York training was followed from 1893 to 1895 by the obligatory stint for English-speaking artists of Morris' generation at the Académie Julian in Paris, where he studied in the *atélier* of Jean-Paul Laurens and Benjamin Constant. He also attended Jean-Léon Gérôme's classes at the Académie des Beaux Arts.[8]

Morris' academic training made him proficient in oils, watercolors and pastels, although from which teachers he learned the most is hard to say. The large classes in the popular academies of the time militated against any close contact between pupils and their teachers. Morris rarely mentions his teachers in his diary except to list them. He thought Gérôme a better sculptor than a painter (although he continued attending his classes after making this observation); and when Morris died he owned three paintings and three prints by his old New York teacher Kenyon Cox.[9]

Morris returned to Canada in 1896 and painted for several summers in and around Ste. Anne de Beaupré with several future members of the Canadian Art Club, including Maurice Cullen, William Brymner, Edmond Dyonnet and Horatio Walker.[10] This area of Quebec, especially Charlevoix County, was a popular painting spot for both Quebec- and Toronto-based artists.[11] Morris was elected an Associate of the Royal Canadian Academy in 1898 and during the next several years held a number of one-man exhibitions at private galleries in Toronto, Ottawa and Montreal.[12] Elected to the Ontario Society of Artists in 1905, he resigned his membership in the OSA in 1907 in order to found the Canadian Art Club. He was the sustaining force behind this organization until his death, although he continued to send paintings to the RCA exhibitions as late as 1912.[13]

The earliest drawings in the exhibition date from 1889-90, when he was studying with Cruikshank in Toronto (cats. 2-6). These are drawings of military subjects with historical interest: the Old Toronto Fort with its blockhouses, canons on the waterfront. In several instances two versions exist of the same subject — the first executed in pencil; the second, with corrections, executed in sepia. These drawings are characterized by a vigorous if slightly dry execution that marks them as the product of an artist with promise. Because they were executed while Morris was a student, it seems likely that Cruikshank had Morris essay the same subject in different media.

There are no known works from his years of study abroad. The earliest painting in the exhibition is *Girls in a Poppy Field* (AGO, cat. 1), which was executed in Holland in 1895.[14] At the same time he painted *Spinning,* which was purchased in 1898 by the Ontario Government. This work was destroyed by fire in the 1950s, but is known from photographs (fig. 1). Both these works are couched in the prevailing stylistic idioms of the period, particularly contemporary Hague School work.[15]

Characteristic of the artists of this school is a tendency to use sombre, closely-allied values in an overall harmony, and a penchant for pastoral landscapes.

Fig. 1   Edmund Morris, *Spinning* (purchased by the Ontario Government and destroyed by fire in the 1950s). This painting may have been originally titled *Dutch Interior*.

Fig. 2   Albert Neuhuys (1844 - 1914)
Winding Wool, 1874
oil on canvas, 317/8 × 477/8 (81 × 121)
Enschede, Rijksmuseum Twenthe

We know from exhibition lists what kind of paintings Morris was executing after his return to Canada in 1896, although only a handful of these have resurfaced. He exhibited both Canadian landscapes and scenes sketched on his European jaunts. A 1902 trip to Scotland provided him with a rich font of compositions, and Scottish scenes appear in his exhibitions for many years thereafter. It appears that he was painting with an eye sharpened by sketching picturesque scenes in Europe, and he looked for compositions with the same pictorial value when painting in Canada, which may explain his preference for the lower Quebec landscape.

This lack of securely-dated works from the period 1896 to c. 1903 means that it has not proved possible to compare Morris' paintings executed during these years to those painted by his Quebec-based artist friends Cullen, Brymner and Dyonnet. Such a comparison would be highly desirable, given that these artists painted together so often in the late 1890s. However, it is possible to compare a slightly later Morris to a painting by Cullen. In 1905 Morris executed a pastel of *L'Anse-des-Mères* (NGC, fig. 4) which is remarkably similar to a 1904 Cullen painting of the same subject (Musée du Quebec, fig. 3). Since both works are securely dated, the Cullen a year earlier than the Morris, this demonstrates clearly that as late as 1905 Cullen and Morris were painting in a very similar manner. This makes it seem likely that they were painting in a similar vein in earlier years. If this were true, dated works by Cullen could be used cautiously to help date works by Morris. Four small panels by Morris (cats. 7-10) lend themselves to this dating by reference to Cullen's work. Their coloration — predominantly greens, browns and ochres — are precisely the same as the range found in such Cullen works as his 1896 *Spring Thaw* (p.c., color illus. on p. 23 of Cullen catalogue). They are similar in style, too, especially as regards their treatment of a pastoral landscape. On this basis, the four Morris panels could be assigned a c. 1896 date and at least some idea of Morris' style during the years immediately following his return to Canada could be gleaned.

I am chary of drawing too many inferences on this evidence — especially concerning Cullen's possible influence on Morris. The two views of *L'Anse-des-Mères* show clearly that Cullen influenced Morris' choice of subject. But does a shared subject necessarily mean that Cullen influenced Morris' style as well? While it is quite possible that Cullen did influence Morris, the evidence does not permit of an unequivocal judgement. The question may be answered more definitely as more works by Morris from this period turn up, but until then the most reasonable assertion is that both artists shared a general debt to the prevailing stylistic idiom of the period.

Morris also exhibited Indian portraits during these years. Their earliest mention comes in 1894, when he exhibited a now-lost painting titled *Portrait of an Iroquois*.[16] Another *Portrait of an Indian* (fig. 5), which may have been executed from a photograph of a Pueblo or Navajo Indian, seems on stylistic grounds to be quite early. Its highly finished surface and laboured technique are aeons away from his later Indian portraits, which are much looser in handling. The work also has a generalized and caricatural aspect that is very different from his later Indian portraits which respect each sitter's individuality.

Fig. 3   Maurice Cullen, *L'Anse-des-Mères,* 1904
oil on canvas, 56 15/16 × 69 3/8 (144.6 × 176.2)
Musée du Québec

Fig. 4   Edmund Morris, *Quebec,* 1905
pastel on paper, 10 7/16 × 14 3/16 (26.5 × 35.6)
National Gallery of Canada, Ottawa.

Fig.5 Edmund Morris, *Portrait of an Indian,*
c. 1894
oil on board, 8 × 10 (20.3 × 25.4)
Harold Groves, King City

Morris exhibited other Indian portraits between 1900 and 1905. Whether these were executed from photographs or from life is unknown. In a 1905 exhibition held in Ottawa, Morris exhibited Indian costumes along with his portraits; these had been presented to his father many years previously.

Also included in his exhibitions of c. 1905 were numerous portraits of a genre-like nature, mainly of habitants and sailors. Typical of these portraits is his *Portrait of a Habitant* (cat. 11), which, although undated, would seem to correspond to descriptions of works exhibited in 1905, although it could well be from an earlier date.

The pastel of the habitant, dark-toned and moody, is a sensitive and evocative portrait which shows Morris' facility in pastel even before he undertook his Indian portraits. He represents the slightly-wary young man in his native dress, sitting stiffly and ill-at-ease in a dark interior. Behind him on the wall hangs a gun with a powder horn slung beside it.

During the years 1903 - 1905 he painted some of his strongest landscapes, including *Cap Tourmente* (NGC, cat. 12) and *Cove Fields, Quebec* (NGC, cat. 14). These show all the hallmarks of his mature style: a bravura handling of paint; a tendency to use a restricted palette with a number of closely-allied hues; a reduction of extraneous narrative so that the viewer's attention is focused only on the vast expanse of the landscape.

It was also during the period 1896 - 1904 that he participated in international exhibitions; *Cap Tourmente,* for instance, was exhibited in the St. Louis Universal Exposition in 1904. He had earlier sent works to the Berlin International in 1896, the Glasgow International in 1901, and Buffalo's Pan-American Exposition in that same year.[17] His *Girls in a Poppy Field* was awarded a bronze medal at the Buffalo Exposition, his highest achievement at one of these international exhibitions.

The year 1906 saw a decisive turning point in his career. He was awarded a commission from the Ontario Government to paint the Ojibway in northern Ontario, and to do so, he accompanied the poet and Indian Affairs Commissioner Duncan Campbell Scott on Treaty Expedition Nine to James Bay.[18] Morris produced a number of sensitive pastel portraits at this time which are now in the collection of the Royal Ontario Museum, Toronto. (Unfortunately, none was available for the exhibition.)

Scott assiduously photographed the Indians while on this trip, and one of the photographs he took shows Morris sketching Chief Cheesequinine at Chapleau, Ontario (fig. 6).[19] Morris would later use a camera extensively on his own Western trips — he took over seven hundred photographs of Indians on the Prairies and of their surroundings — and one memorable photograph (fig. 7) shows White Buffalo Calf standing in front of his half-completed portrait (cat. 24).[20] Morris probably used the photographs as an *aide-mémoire* to assist him in the studio, since there are both Indian portraits and landscapes in the exhibition which appear to have been based on photographs (figs. 22-35).

The 1906 trip also provided him with material for landscapes such as *A Northern River* (cat. 17) and *In the Country of the Ojibway* (Ont. Gov't Coll., fig. 14). The landscapes of this period are characterized by a dark ruddy tonality which is not entirely successful. Morris experimented with a new red ochre ground in these paintings, a technique which he soon abandoned.

Fig. 6   Edmund Morris sketching Chief
Cheesequinine at Chapleau, Ontario 1907
Public Archives Canada/PA59587

Fig. 8   Edmund Morris, *White Buffalo Calf (Child-Unistaipoka),* 1909
(cat. 24)

Fig. 7   *White Buffalo Calf (Child-Unistaipoka)*
Photograph by Edmund Morris, c. 1909
Manitoba Archives, Winnipeg

The 1906 Indian portraits were well-received, and Morris was awarded a second commission from the Ontario government to paint Indians living further west in the province. These commissions led to similar assignments from the Saskatchewan and Alberta governments, and from 1907 to 1910 he made annual trips to Western Canada.[21] The majority of his Indian portraits date from this period.

From 1911 to 1913, his Indian portrait commissions completed, he concentrated once more on landscape. In 1911 he wrote to then Premier Walter Scott of Saskatchewan, "this year I am talking up a work which I regard as important as the portraits — groups of the Indian lodges in the surrounding landscape."[22] He painted several of these; typical is *Indian Encampment on the Prairie* (AGO, cat. 36). He also continued to paint historical subjects, now placing them into a larger landscape context. This is seen in *Old Fort Edmonton* (Glenbow, cat. 15). By 1912, he was painting pure landscapes, such as *A Saskatchewan Landscape* (location unknown, fig. 16), a bleak wilderness landscape handled with verve.[23] In 1913, retracing steps he had taken many years before, he was once more sketching the lower St. Lawrence. There are no known works from the last year of his life.

In general, his work shows little stylistic progression, nor do his subjects change substantially over the years. The characteristics of his mature landscape style are all to be found in *Cap Tourmente,* of c. 1903; it seems little different from a work in 1912, such as *A Saskatchewan Landscape.* The same may be said about his portraits. With the exception of the Indian portrait I have tentatively dated to 1894, Morris' portraits seem remarkably homogeneous in style. Until more works by the artist come to light therefore, only the broadest sketch of his stylistic development can be given.

Morris' work was regarded as unconventional by most reviewers, who either praised it or criticized it for that reason. His quick sketchy technique even prompted one reviewer to ask rhetorically whether several of Morris' oil sketches on view at the Canadian Art Club's 1912 exhibition would even be considered art.[24] The reviewer did not think so. Most reviewers regarded his landscapes in an entirely different light from his portraits; reviewers who preferred the portraits were often the first to criticize the landscapes.

Morris held his first exhibition in Toronto in the spring of 1896 at a private gallery and reviewer Lynne Doyle wrote:

> Nothing so unconventional, showing such vigor and breadth of treatment, has been seen here for some time as the watercolors by Mr. Edmund M. Morris ... in each and all is seen the same simplicity and strength, so that most other work in the room seems tame or 'niggling' in comparison.[25]

In a review of a second Morris exhibition held in the same gallery in the fall of that year, however, Doyle observed that Morris' works were not achieving much popular success, writing, "the art beloved of artists often fails to win the approval of the public, and this may to some extent be the case with the work of ... Morris." The works on view were "so simple as to be only studies, although studies full of suggestiveness." Even though they were "spirited but sketchy," Doyle thought it probable that "each and all are better appreciated at some distance when their best qualities are felt without any idea of 'paint' which closer inspection is apt to bring up."[26]

The points of criticism brought out in this review — Morris' slapdash technique which left viewers with a tangible reminder of the medium and his lack of success with Toronto's art-going public — are representative of the tenor of many reviews of his work. To his credit, Morris never modified his painting to please Toronto's conservative audiences. And if as a consequence he never enjoyed broad-based popularity, at least some reviews offered encouraging words.

In 1901, Morris was reviewed positively in the *International Studio.* The reviewer found that Morris was "most at home in watercolours, his control over this medium being truly remarkable. He has also a true eye for colour, and the quality of his line has strength and charm." The reviewer thought that Morris was "a young man of true art intuition and of strong convictions, and is certain to come to the front in Canadian art," but felt impelled to add, "more especially when maturity shall have given to his brush the power of sureness and of greater coherency."[27]

By 1908, a reviewer in *The Canadian Magazine* described Morris as:

> One of those who has felt the fascination of this country, its vitality, the grimness of its large spaces, the mystery of its waterways and forests and who has deliberately, knowing the cost, determined to make his lifework in his own country.[28]

From 1908 to 1913, when Morris exhibited with the Canadian Art Club, his work usually was relegated to secondary mention following a detailed review of one of the more important artists such as Horatio Walker, Homer Watson or James Wilson Morrice. However, Morris did receive his share of positive exhibition notices while exhibiting with the Club. For instance, E. F. B. Johnston, a Toronto lawyer and stalwart defender of the Club, reviewed Morris' contribution to the Club's inaugural exhibition in 1908 in the following terms:

Fig. 9   Inaugural exhibition of Canadian Art Club, 4 - 17 February 1908, 57 Adelaide Street East, Toronto. *Cap Tourmente* (cat. 12) and *A Northern River* (cat. 17) are included in the present exhibition. See Appendix A for a listing of works that Morris exhibited during his career.

Edmund Morris, a rising and ambitious artist, shows his power of delineating character and representing national types in his admirable painted Indian chiefs, now the property of the Province. The calm, dignified and reserved force of the Indian is convincingly portrayed. The portraits are the result of intelligent observation and reflection. His landscapes are strong, and show a feeling for nature's ruggedness, which is refreshing in these days of too much prettiness in pictures. His pictures are entirely unconventional, and indicate an originality of conception and execution rarely met with in the work of a young man. Here and there one comes across a touch of the poetry of art, but his pictures appeal more to the sense of strength and vitality of truth than to the ideal.[29]

The reviewer for *The World* held a similar opinion, writing of Morris' Indian portraits in the 1908 Club show:

Such pastel work has rarely been seen in Toronto. With all the delicacy of that kind of painting it combines a strength which lifts it into a higher region of art and stamps its author as an original genius of no little promise.[30]

Fig. 10 Installation of the Morris Collection of Indian Portraits and Artifacts at the Gallery of the Canadian Art Club, 57 Adelaide Street East, Toronto, 29 March - 17 April 1909.

Morris held a solo exhibition in 1909 which consisted exclusively of Indian portraits and implements. He wrote a small pamphlet which accompanied the exhibition.[31] Byron E., later Sir Edmund Walker, the Toronto art-connoisseur and banker, reviewed the exhibition. He wrote:

> I do not need to tell you that those portraits by Mr. Morris are quite different from the often veracious but always inartistic portraits of Indians by most other painters. These are works of art, as delightful in color as they are vigorous in drawing and searching in analysis of Indian character.[32]

The same exhibition received favorable notice in the New-York based *American Art News,* an indication that Morris was beginning to attract international attention.[33] When the same portraits were shown at the Canadian Art Club's 1909 exhibition, they attracted similarly favorable mention. The reviewer in the *Canadian Courier* wrote, "Mr. Edmund Morris has a brave corner all to himself, where hang such splendid warriors as 'Big Darkness' and 'A Saulteaux Chief'. They are mighty heads, painted with a spirit and dignity which is admirable."[34] James Mavor, the University of Toronto economics professor who was very active in local art circles, described the portraits as "vigorous and faithful renderings of remarkable types of which it is very advisable to preserve authentic records."[35]

Other reviewers were willing to concede the historical importance of Morris' Indian portraits, but they were not sure if they liked them all that much. A reviewer writing in a local university paper, the *Acta Victoriana,* referred to Morris' "important but not altogether pleasing ethnological labor on the Indians," while a reviewer writing in the *Canadian Courier* in 1911 wrote that the Indian portraits were "historically valuable but not necessarily popular."[36]

The landscapes also attracted mixed reviews. The reviewer in *Saturday Night,* after seeing Morris' paintings in the 1911 Club exhibition, wrote, "the treatment is severe to the point of harshness, and the colours are heavy, without a trace of brilliancy and vibrating qualities one expects in western scenery," although he conceded they did have "a certain unconventional vigor and sincerity which gives them an interest all their own."[37] A reviewer of the Club's 1912 exhibition described some of Morris' quick sketches as "very highly impressionistic," concluding, "they are striking, but are they art?"[38]

The reviewers who liked Morris' landscapes praise him for his "vigor and insight," "vivid yet true coloring and ... skillfull arrangement." They note the "strong contrast of color, which rises at times to a remarkable brilliancy."[39] Even Hector Charlesworth, perhaps Toronto's most conservative critic, grudgingly acknowledged during a review of Morris' posthumous contribution to the Club's 1914 exhibition, "the group of works by the late Edmund Morris, while they do not bear very close inspection, as seen from the distance show fine imaginative grasp and power in composition."[40]

The lukewarm tribute Charlesworth paid Morris in his review signals how rapidly Morris fell even from the small pinnacles to which his reputation had climbed. Although Newton MacTavish, in his book *The Fine Arts in Canada,* published in 1925, recognized Morris as an important organizer among Toronto's artists, he gave a short shrift to his art.[41] Morris briefly resurfaced in 1928, when the Art Gallery of Toronto held a memorial exhibition in order to sell the paintings Morris had bequeathed to the Ontario College of Art.[42] But the prices realized for many of his paintings were pitiful — ranging from $3 to $24.[43]

Probably the first stirrings of interest in Morris since then came from Dennis Reid, who in *A Concise History of Canadian Painting* published in 1973 devoted a chapter to the Canadian Art Club and Morris' role in it.[44] Since that time scholarly research has proceeded on a number of different fronts, with the possibility of a biography on Morris appearing shortly, as well as the transcription and publication of his nearly-illegible diaries.[45]

Given such a broad-based revival of interest in Morris as a person, therefore, it seems appropriate to ask, after the nearly three-quarters of a century since his death, just how good a painter was he? The Indian portraits stand up well. They are superior to anything produced by his close contemporaries.[46] Executed with a pleasing freshness and freedom from convention, they are non-sentimental and at times, such as in the portrait of Blackfoot Chief *Iron Shield* (NGC, fig. 11), achieve a monumentality that raises them to heroic scale.

Fig. 11   Edmund Morris, *The Blackfoot Chief Ironshield,* 1907
pastel on paper, 25¼ × 20½ (64.2 × 52.1)
National Gallery of Canada, Ottawa
Gift from the artist's estate, 1922

A characteristic of Morris' portraiture is that he maintains a certain distance from his sitters. In the *Portait of a Habitant,* for example (cat. 11), despite his accurate rendering of the man's physiognomy, he does not impart to the study a psychological dimension. He remains a recorder of the surface appearance of the figure rather than attempting to capture the interior motivations of the sitter. His approach to portraiture may be compared to his contemporary George Reid (1860 - 1947), whose representations of figures with similar domestic interiors are often imbued with a heavy-handed social commentary. His well-known *Mortgaging the Homestead* (NGC) is an example. In comparison, Morris — even with this subject as redolent of genre as this view of a young man living a life whose time had long since passed — refuses to make the figure a larger symbol. Generally speaking, this is true of all his portraits. Morris never uses an individual to make a statement with larger social overtones.

As a consequence of this approach, Morris distances himself from the underlying social implications in all his portraits, including those of Indians. We may regret this to a certain extent, because we can not read from his portraits what he believed. Yet precisely *because* Morris remains aloof from his subjects, in the end his portraits are more successful than had he succumbed to the allure of showing the tragedy of the Indians' plight. To do so would have left pathos teetering dangerously near the precipice beyond which lies bathos. By eschewing a moral stance in his portraits, Morris allows the viewer to make up his own mind about the underlying implications of what he sees.

With regard to his landscapes, I am inclined to agree with many of his early reviewers, who typically termed his work "spirited and sketchy", and "full of promise". Like them, I admire his verve in handling; but also like them, I feel that not all his landscapes achieved the full expression of his early promise. Still, the best Morris landscapes can approach the monumental scale of his Indian portraits. *Cap Tourmente* has already been cited as an example of Morris' mature landscape style. The subject was not new; indeed, almost the same view had been engraved during the nineteenth century in such books as *The Shoe and Canoe,* a description of travel in Lower Canada published in 1850 (fig. 12).[47] But in comparison to the tame engraving, Morris' version of this scene brings drama into the landscape.

In Morris' smaller landscapes, especially the cigar-box-sized *pochades* such as *Indian Tepees: Manitoba* (cat. 37), the bravura brushwork seen in the foreground of *Cap Tourmente* is applied even more freshly; the same subtle varied palette is found; and once more the richly-textured surface is juxtaposed against a deep pictorial space.

Morris did not always achieve such spontaneous results in his work, however; to my eyes, and I suspect others' as well, many of his landscapes appear overworked and too dark. This is true of a work such as *A Northern River* (Ont. Gov't. Coll., cat. 17). A comparison between the preparatory pastel sketch (cat. 16) and the finished canvas shows how much darker Morris made the oil. One strains to pick out the details which seem to be lost in the shadowy depths. This dark effect is accentuated by his painting technique. In *The Country of the Ojibway* (Ont. Gov't. Coll., fig. 14) Morris' red

Fig. 12 *Les Eboulements — from below Cape
Tourment* Engraving from John J. Bigsby, *The
Shoe and Canoe, or Pictures of Travel in the
Canadas* 1850, Vol. I, opp. p. 185, Metropolitan Toronto Library.

Fig. 13 Edmund Morris, *Cap Tourmente,* c. 1903
(cat. 12)

ochre ground is allowed to show through the surface. Other portions of the canvas are worked up through numerous layers of opaque pigment.

In defense of Morris' dark palette, however, it is worth remarking that Morris' diary for 1906 contains numerous color notes which show that he actually was quite accurate in his color range, even in his darkest paintings. On one occasion he writes, "trees of umber colour, a little grey ground, black and ash colour, grey trunks of trees," and on another he writes, "I paint the grey-green of moss on trees."[48] Other color notes seem to describe quite faithfully the range of tones in *A Northern River,* such as when he writes, "trees very dark — water muddy olive brown reflecting silver white on the side — blue of sky — light on black heads. Here also, light on the Indians' faces, the colours very luminous and yellow red," and in one last instance, he observes, "rocks warm like brown; red streaks and at the base of water line deep blue reflecting the sky."[49] And it is possible that the paintings have darkened since they were executed. In a 1906 installation exhibition photo (fig. 9), *A Northern River* appeared much lighter that it is today.

Morris' limited tonal range is more varied than it appears at first glance. A work such as the probably-misnamed *Last Light* (AGH, cat. 13) exhibits this to perfection. The range of colors in it is marvellously subtle, with hues ranging from umber to pure chrome yellow, from turquoise to ultramarine. The warm ground imparts a richness to the painting which is complemented by red highlights covered in brown. The painting glows like a just-dormant volcano.

Fig. 14   Edmund Morris, *In the Country of the Ojibway,* 1906
oil on canvas, 29½ × 39 (74.9 × 99.1)
Ontario Government Collection
Gift of the Artist 1906

It is true though that many of Morris' large landscapes adhere to a parcel of consistent and repetitive compositional formulae: a dark repoussoir element in the foreground is juxtaposed against a distant infinite landscape; the middle ground links the fore- and background by means of a diagonal receding into depth. Often this diagonal is a river. Above, a bruise-hued sky rent by jagged sunlit openings casts an uneven, dramatic light.

Any discussion of Morris' landscapes would be incomplete without discussing his stylistic debts to other artists and schools. In fact, Morris' style reveals a veritable stew of the previous fifty years or so of European art, with pungent traces from Holland, particularly the Hague School.[50] The Hague School, distantly inspired by the great landscape painters of Holland's Golden Age in the seventeenth century, and more closely inspired by the French Barbizon painters of the mid-nineteenth century, was the most important influence in Canada besides Impressionism, and was especially attractive to collectors.[51] Morris was doubtless familiar with Hague School work, since he had painted in Holland during the summer of 1895.[52] *Girls in a Poppy Field* was executed that year while in Holland, and its debt to Dutch painting contemporary with it is clear. Should any additional proof of his debt to the Hague School be needed, it is readily found in his now-destroyed painting *Spinning* (fig. 1). This is comparable in style and in mood to any Dutch paintings of interior scenes, such as Albert Neuhuys' *Winding Wool,* of 1874 (fig. 2). Canadian artists had been painting such domestic genre interiors for some time, as witnessed by George Reid's 1888 *Gossip* (AGO).

Fig. 15   William Langson Lathrop (1859 - 1938)
The Muskrat Hunter, 1893
oil on canvas, 30 × 40 (74.9 × 101.6)
Reading Public Museum and Art Gallery

Fig. 16   Edmund Morris, *A Saskatchewan Landscape,* c. 1912
oil on canvas, (Present location unknown)

The style of Morris' landscapes seem to have a good deal in common with the Hague School, but are actually closer in spirit to contemporary American work.[53] A painter such as William Langson Lathrop (1859-1938) shares with Morris a stark and simplified vision which has little in common with the domestic and pastoral landscapes typical of Hague School artists. A Lathrop painting titled *The Muskrat Hunter,* dated 1893 (fig. 15), shows the same vast expanse of sky and infinite, almost frightening depth as Morris' *A Saskatchewan Landscape* (fig. 16), dated 1912. Since artists such as Lathrop were themselves influenced stylistically by the Hague School and the Barbizon tradition, it is interesting to see that they should arrive at a similar vision of nature to that of Morris, although achieved independently.

It is important to realize just how dominant this tonal approach to painting was among Canadian painters during this period. And while tonal painting is particularly associated with Morris and his colleagues in the Canadian Art Club, future members of the Group of Seven were also painting in this manner. A. Y. Jackson's *Bruges* (Kleinburg, McMichael Collection), painted in 1908, is a muddy-hued work that is tamer and less accomplished than a Morris painted at this time. Jackson painted other works in this vein, as late as 1912, such as *Assisi* (AGO). Adapting the tonal approach to Canadian landscape, future Group member J. E. H. Macdonald painted such works as *By the River, Early Spring,* 1911 (Ont. Gov't Coll.), and the 1912 *Early Evening, Winter* (AGO).

In other words, Morris' tonal paintings should not be regarded with eyes made severe by several generations of earnest Canadian landscape painters. It is not fair to criticize him simply because he did not break through the prevailing stylistic idioms of the period. For to follow this line of reasoning — that Morris and other tonal painters were only precursors of the Group — leads one onto boggy intellectual fields. We are on shifting ground if we assert that the Group broke through the fetters of the foreign styles epitomized by the painting technique of Morris. Not only does such a position go against the evidence — because manifestly the future members of the Group painted with the same tonal palette as Morris — but then we must define as a 'breakthrough' the replacing of Dutch tonalism characteristic of Morris with Fauve-colored Scandanavian Impressionism mixed with traces of international *art nouveau.* And does Algonquin Park serve as a more potent symbol of the Canadian psyche than the great northwest? Who knows if Morris would have adapted his palette to meet the changing perception of the Canadian landscape if his career had not been so tragically cut off?

Morris' career as a painter is naturally the most important focus of this exhibition, but his other activities should also be considered, primarily his literary efforts and role with the Canadian Art Club. If from his father Morris inherited a deep respect for Canada's native peoples, he also inherited an even deeper respect for the importance of history. The young Morris grew up with a firm conviction that what his family was doing was important; even as a child he began to keep a diary. I have already quoted liberally from Morris' early diaries, all of which have survived. They provide valuable insights into his development.

Given Morris' passion for historical record, it is ironic that much of the written record he has left is of extremely limited value. One problem is his nearly illegible handwriting. His friend the poet Duncan Campbell Scott once described in a poem, a letter he received from Morris as "your famous scribble,/It was ever a cryptic fist,/Cuneiform or Chaldaic/Meanings held in a mist."[54]

Morris' earliest diary, kept in a pocket-sized leather-bound note book, the entries dashed off in a violent scrawl, records the years from 1886 to 1904. In it Morris is more informative about train and ship departure times that he is about artistic matters. His style is telegraphic and many entries are written well after the fact. Entries are haphazardly dated. As a result of this casual attitude to dating and particulars, many questions about his student days are unanswerable. For example, we rarely know when he meets someone. Maurice Cullen and William Brymner's names simply appear one day. When did he meet Morrice?[55] What did he think of Parisian art? Unanswerable. His diary does reveal that his taste in art was conventional. He was drawn to the Anglo-American circle around Whistler rather than to modern French painters. The names of English artists, such as Tryon, Romney and Constable frequently appear; Frank Brangwyn's name is cited no less than four times. The only French artist singled out for praise is Manet, of whose *Boy with a Sword* Morris writes that he will "never forget."[56] There is only one instance when he reveals an interest in what now might be termed "progressive" art. This is when in 1896 he records that "I went to Murton Abbey in Surrey to see William Morris' works — saw his process of making tapestries — dyeing silks and wools — I was unable to see him."[57]

Fig. 17 *Poling — Abitibi River,* 1906
Photograph taken during 1906 Treaty Expedition
Nine to James Bay. Compare to *Indians Descending the Pic River* (cat. 16) and *A Northern River* (cat. 17)
Photo: Ontario Archives, Toronto

With the 1906 commission from the Ontario government in hand, Morris began a new diary — this one fortunately as full of details as his earlier one had been of ship schedules. He records matter-of-factly the general squalor of Ontario's Indians then living in the north. It is sometimes difficult to reconcile the passionate stories he records with the neutral tone he accords them. Much as in his portraits, he remains a detached observer. He notes without comment that the commission's canoes leaked constantly, and that they had to face constant rain and waves of flies. By the middle of August — the trip started at the beginning of the month — he starts to make quick sketches in his notebook, sometimes with detailed color notes added to them (fig. 18-19). He becomes fascinated with the subtle gradations of the landscape.

This diary was followed by another which records the years 1907 to 1910, when his life revolved around the great cycle of his western journeys. The diary now has a self-conscious tone that makes it look as if he intended publishing it at some point — he refers to himself on occasion as 'this writer' and talks about books in a learned manner — but the resulting stiffness of tone is more than offset by the rich trove of material that he records: Indian legends, bits of gossip, quick sketches of Indian implements. He was given an Indian name, and he records the occasion laconically:

Fig. 18   Edmund Morris, *Diary for 1886 - 1904*,
approx. p. 37
Landscape with colour notes
Queen's University Archives, Kingston

Fig. 19   Edmund Morris, *Diary for 1886 - 1904,*
approx. pp. 24-25.
Landscape with colour notes
Queen's University Archives, Kingston

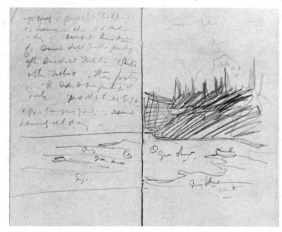

The chief named me Kyaiyii, Bear Robe, after a great Blackfoot chief he had heard of as a boy. He requested me to take a message to the great chief at Ottawa. All the old chiefs have the same to say. They do not want any part of the reserve sold. The promise was given them at the Treaty and if broken will remain as a dark spot in our history.[58]

Painting Indians required its own approach, as we find out. Morris resolved to paint *Iron Shield* (fig. 11), whom he described as "haughty, and his bearing looks the King", even though everyone who knew the chief said he would never consent to being painted.[59] Morris did get the chief's consent but only after being subjected to a tirade against the government in Ottawa. When he finally started the portrait, Morris recorded:

all went well till late in the afternoon. This Indian work is unlike ordinary portrait work where we have sittings for two hours at a time. They are impatient & want to get it done & sit like statues, never resting — so I keep them at it according to their wish. I had advised Iron Shield to rest but he would not & at last jumped up with a yell, tore off his buckskin clothes, tossed them aside & stalked away. I got my interpreter & asked what the trouble was. He said nothing so I gave up & started away. He then got sorry & came out. I shook hands & said I would come & finish it next day.[60]

Experiences such as these, multiplied many times over, gave Morris an expertise in Indian thinking. He was probably more sympathetic to their problems than most white men of the period. He was quick to condemn attempts to quash the free practice of their religion, and willingly entered the debate then raging about the future of Canadian Indians. Morris' solution, as proposed in a letter to the *Winnipeg Free Press* in 1910, called for the establishment of India-style regiments of native soldiers to offset the numbing effects of reservation life.[61]

Back home in Toronto, Morris was equally quick to propose solutions as to how to improve the fortunes of art in that city.[62] He helped found the Art Museum of Toronto, and served on its executive. In addition, Morris was pursuing his own painting career, writing a book on early Canadian artists, sending aggrieved letters about proposals to pass over Canadian artists in favor of French sculptors for a monument to the War of 1812, and writing biographical queries to anyone with any connection to Canadian art.[63] He also found time to write *Art in Canada: The Early Painters,* published in 1911, one of the first books on Canadian art history. But his most significant contribution was to serve as secretary of the Toronto-based Canadian Art Club which, from its founding in 1907, occupied most of Morris' considerable energies. He did not complain about his role, but a remark to Premier Walter Scott of Saskatchewan indicates the extent to which organizing for the Club ate into his time. In a letter dated 6 March 1911 - five months after receiving a letter from Scott — he wrote:

[t]he work of bringing about our Canadian Art Club exhibition has been on my shoulders and in consequence my correspondence has got behind, but the exhibition is a great success and if you saw it I am sure you would think the effort worthwhile.[64]

Fig. 20   Members of the Canadian Art Club
Standing l. to r.: A. Phimister Proctor,   Seated l. to r.: Horatio Walker, W. E. Atkinson,
       Walter Allward, Curtis Williamson   J. Archibald Browne
       Edmund Morris   Photo: Art Gallery of Ontario

On his shoulders it was: it seems unlikely that the organization could have existed without his drive and perseverence. Fortunately, Morris was just as scrupulous in preserving the records of the Club as he was in preserving his own diaries. He saved every scrap of paper associated with the Club — from its invoices to frank heated exchanges between Club members — tipping the letters and documents into a set of hefty leather-bound scrapbooks now housed in the Art Gallery of Ontario. Throughout the scrapbooks, Morris, in his impossible chickenscratch, soothes ruffled feathers, cajoles, badgers, informs and proseletyses. The scrapbooks testify to Morris' perseverence, his integrity, and his never-say-quit attitude to organizing.

It appears he was likeable and liked, probably for just those qualities of enthusiasm and sincerity that characterize his correspondence. He also had a flair for the unexpected. During his 1909 exhibition of Indian artifacts held at the Club galleries, for instance, he wrote in his diary, "the closing night I gave a smoker, inviting my men friends. Horatio Walker and [A. P.] Procter came up from New York for it. As we were breaking up I struck the tomtom and Proctor and I gave the War dance!''[65] Morris was clearly the heart and soul of the Club. Neither temperate nor reasoned, but impetuous and excitable with his own inimitable style, these qualities were used to good effect. In retrospect, a better secretary for the Club could not have been chosen. Morris called on his wide circle of acquaintances in Europe and Canada, his knowledge of many different exhibiting societies and their policies — and when it came to recruiting new members, rarely took no for an answer.

To enlist A. P. Proctor as a Club member, for instance — the same Proctor with whom Morris danced the war dance — Morris writes to Horatio Walker in New York early in 1909, asking Walker to contact Proctor.[66] Proctor, born in Ontario but raised in the Western United States and then living in New York, was a realist sculptor of animals then at the peak of his reputation. The tigers he sculpted for Princeton University in 1909 won the Gold Medal of the Architectural League of New York that year.

Walker contacts Proctor, and much to his surprise Proctor is enthusiastic about the possibility of exhibiting in his native country. (Walker had termed Proctor "a canayen ... who thinks there is no good in the country.")[67] Proctor then writes Morris, saying he will join the Club: "it is very nice of you to wish me to join and I appreciate it very much." He concludes, "I am exceedingly pleased to have some of my things shown in my native country, where nothing of mine has ever been seen."[68] Proctor sent a number of bronzes to the Club's 1909 show, and came up for the opening of the exhibition. Proctor apparently liked very much what he saw, since in a letter to Morris from the train back to New York dated 25 April 1909, he writes, "I have come back full of enthusiasm for the C.A.C. and belief [sic] that *we're off* and that we'll make things hum. We must keep the *next exhibition* in our minds and work every day for it. 'Shoot-em-up' so fast and hard they'll know we're in town for sure."[69]

By 1911, Morris and Proctor had become fast friends, brought together by a love of Western Canada. Proctor — once described by journalist and art-chronicler Newton MacTavish as "always very serious in demeanor, apparently only concerned with art" — addresses Morris by his Indian name 'Kyaiyii' and 'old pal' in correspondence that is as salty as it is spontaneous.[70] They take several trips to the West together, and Proctor remained a faithful exhibitor with the Club, sending works every year until its folding in 1915.

It is apparent from this example how much of the Club's success in recruiting artists such as Proctor depended on the gregarious and likeable Morris. What is more significant, however, is that once having made a firm friend and ally in Proctor, Morris used him in the same way he had used Walker — to enlist other members in New York. Proctor writes Morris, 22 April 1913 "Have been talking with Royal Cortissoz — he said he was very proud to accept honorary membership in the C.A.C."[71] Cortissoz, a leading New York art critic who was in 1913 both literary and art editor for the *New York Herald Tribune,* also wrote extensively and well in many books on American art, architecture and sculpture. His book of essays titled *Art and*

Common Sense was published in 1913 and later reached four editions. He was therefore an important tactical addition to the Club's laymembership, a person of critical acuity and international experience. Then, on 29 April 1913, Proctor writes Morris to suggest honorary membership for August Jacacci, "who knows a heap about art," as Proctor put it.[72] Jacacci, while not in Cortissoz's league, was also a New York-based writer on art. Morris must have written Jacacci immediately on receipt of Proctor's letter, because on 6 May Jacacci writes Morris thanking him for the honor of being asked to be a member.[73] Both Jacacci and Cortissoz were shown in the Club's 1913 catalogue as lay members, a clear indication that the Club's activities were becoming known to an international audience with some influence.

Based on the exchange of letters leading to Proctor's enthusiastic participation in Club exhibitions, and then his own efforts to enlist other members from New York, it is clear that the Club had as a policy the recruitment of an international membership of artists with high reputations, such as Proctor, and also actively courted as laymembers such prominent figures in the international art community as Cortissoz and Jacacci. This exchange also provides an excellent example of Morris' generally-successful recruitment techniques when contacting artists with any connection to Canada. Morris employed similar techniques to enlist other artists with similarly exiguous ties to Canada as Proctor's were, artists such as Ernest Lawson, John Russell and James Kerr Lawson.[74]

Kerr Lawson's reaction when Morris contacted him shows how pleased he was to have an opportunity to exhibit in Canada. In a letter dated 8 January 1912, Kerr Lawson writes Morris:

> It is true I am, like so many of the best Canadians, only a Scotsman by the accident of birth. I had quite intended to enter the world by way of Canada but the dilatory proceedings of my parents made this impracticable. However I think I made good the defect and ... became intensely Canadian and have remained so ever since.[75]

To the Paris-based Club members, such as Clarence Gagnon and James Wilson Morrice, Morris was their only link with Toronto. Typically, Gagnon writes Morris from Paris 22 January 1910 thanking Morris for news: "you are the only one who has been kind enough to give me news of the Club and I appreciate it very much."[76] On another occasion, in 1913, Gagnon writes, "if it was not for the Club I doubt if I should be sending anything to Canada at all, as one gets so little encouragement from one's own country."[77]

It is also probable that without the Club — and without Morris' hand at its helm — Morrice's work would not have been seen in Toronto (with the exception of isolated RCA and OSA exhibitions). Morrice was another faithful Club exhibitor, and he clearly thought that Club exhibitions were superior to anything else that Toronto had to offer.[78] Morrice also considered Morris a good friend, and even considered going with him in the summer of 1908 to paint the Indians in western Canada.[79]

It is clear from these examples how important Morris was to the success of the Canadian Art Club. The documents he preserved speak for themselves, a testament to his contribution to Canadian art. His indefatigable efforts to bring home expatriate artists to exhibit their work in Canada, his ability to break down the traditional barriers between Quebec and Toronto painters, his dynamic organizing abilities, his sincere interest in making history come alive to his generation — in each of these efforts he had no peer. It would be an error though to assess his contribution to Canadian art solely on the basis of these laudable but non-artistic criteria. His own paintings are among the most progressive of his generation; they deserve to be better known.

In 1915, Duncan Campbell Scott published by way of tribute to his friend a long panegyric titled "Lines in Memory of Edmund Morris."[80] The sonorous and sensitive poem evokes their shared times together on the Prairies, especially during the magical crepuscular hours. When I reread it recently, three lines leapt from the page in an unexpected but fitting tribute to Morris. They read:

> Persistence is the master of this life;
> The master of these little lives of ours;
> To the end — effort — even beyond the end.

Geoffrey Simmins

NOTES

1. The best general introduction to Edmund Morris is found in Dennis Reid, *A Concise History of Canadian Painting* (Toronto: Oxford University Press, 1973), pp. 118-134. For the early bibliography on Morris, see Colin S. Macdonald, *Dictionary of Canadian Artists* (Ottawa: Canadian Paperbacks Publishing Ltd. 1974), IV, pp. 1297-98. Articles written since then include Jean McGill, "The Indian Portraits of Edmund Morris," *The Beaver* (Summer 1979), pp. 34-41, and by the same author, "Edmund Morris Among the Saskatchewan Indians and the Fort Qu'Appelle Monument," *Saskatchewan History* XXXV, No. 3 (Autumn 1982), 101-107.

    Morris left a dense accumulation of papers, including diaries, scrapbooks and newspaper clippings. The greatest amount of material is found in Toronto's Art Gallery of Ontario Reference Library, which houses the bulk of the documentation relating to the Canadian Art Club (CAC) and Morris' involvement with this organization. Here is found much of the Club's correspondence, as yet uncatalogued and only very roughly organized. It was compiled by Morris from 1907 until his death in 1913. The correspondence is kept in two letterbooks (hereafter cited as the Morris letterbooks) and in a box of loose correspondence (hereafter cited as the Stone Bequest, after Edgar J. Stone, who donated the letters to the AGO in 1953) This material is supplemented by a book marked "Invoices" which contains newspaper reviews of CAC exhibitions, as well as Morris' own exhibitions, (hereafter cited as Morris "Invoice" book, and by two more scrapbooks which Morris compiled on Canadian artist Wyatt Eaton. In addition, there are twenty-seven letters from James Wilson Morrice to Morris dating from 1897 to 1911; these are in Morrice's artist's file. In the AGO Archives are letters between Morris' brother William and George Reid, then president of the Ontario College of Art, concerning the disposition of 119 paintings which Morris bequeathed to the OCA in order to found a scholarship. The Archives also contain a list of books and works of art which Morris owned at the time of his death, and a short appreciation of Morris which Reid wrote. Reid quotes extensively from Morris' will, which left generous legacies to many Canadian collections (see Appendix B). The will was printed in the *Toronto Telegram,* 27 February 1914; a copy of this is found in Morris' artist's file.

    Morris' early diaries, one covering the years 1886-1904, the other the year 1906, are housed in the Archives of Queen's University, Kingston. Morris' Western Diary, covering the years 1907-1910, is in the collection of the Ethnology Department, Royal Ontario Museum, Toronto. The ROM also has copies of the early diaries, and all of these including the Western Diary have been transcribed by ROM research assistant Mary Fitz-Gibbon. I am indebted to her for access to this material. The Queen's University Archives also contain material relating to a projected history of Perth which Morris compiled. These diaries will be cited hereafter as EMM, *Early Diary,* EMM, *1906 Diary,* and EMM, *Western Diary.* Date and page numbers will be given if Morris provides this information.

    The Ontario Archives in Toronto house the Morris family papers, especially those of Morris' well-known father, Alexander. Also in the Ontario Archives are the papers of the Ontario Society of Artists, whose minute books and correspondence files contain material relating to the resignation of Morris and other future CAC members from the OSA.

    Because of his prominence in Canadian art circles, Morris is mentioned frequently in the papers of some of his Toronto contemporaries. Among these contemporaries are Duncan Campbell Scott, whose papers are in the Thomas

Fisher Rare Book Library, University of Toronto. Also in this repository are the papers of Sir Edmund Walker and James Mavor, two prominent figures in the Toronto arts community at this time. Morris is also mentioned in correspondence between Scott and his friend Pelham Edgar; this correspondence is found in Edgar's papers now in the Victoria University Library, Toronto. Morris is also mentioned in correspondence between Morrice and Newton MacTavish, whose papers are in the Canadiana Collection, North York Public Library (MacTavish's photo collection, donated to the AGO in 1976 by his son Lachlan, contains several photographs of Morris with other CAC members).

There are isolated copses of material on Morris on the Prairies. In the Manitoba Archives in Winnipeg are letters between Morris and then Premier of Saskatchewan, Walter Scott, concerning Morris' commission to paint Indian portraits for the Legislative Building in Regina. The Manitoba Archives also include much additional material, including more newspaper clippings and reviews of Morris' exhibition of Indian portraits; most important in this collection are the negatives of over seven hundred photographs which Morris took of Indians on the Plains and their tepees. Additional photographic material relating to Morris is cited in note 19.

2. In addition to a sepia drawing of Fort York, dated 1890 (cat. 3), there are three other undated and unsigned pencil drawings by Morris in the collection of the Women's Canadian Historical Society, Toronto. According to the Society's archivist, Lorna Procter, Morris donated all these drawings to the Society in 1904, when he became a member. All of the drawings are untitled, but two have attached plaques apparently added later. One plaque reads, "Mennonite settlement, Manitoba, at the Time of Lord Dufferin's and Lieut.-Governor Morris' Visit 1875." The second reads, "Silver Heights, Manitoba, 1873, residence of Lord Strathcona." The third drawing is a view of an unidentified fort.

3. EMM, *Early Diary,* 1888 p. 3.

4. EMM, *Early Diary,* 22 October 1886, p. 1.

5. EMM, *Early Diary,* December 1888, p. 4.

6. EMM, *Early Diary,* [1889] p. 6.

7. Morris lists his teachers on a biographical data form dated 31 December 1912, now in the artist's file in the AGO. It is clear from several letters from A. P. Proctor to Morris, however, that Morris did not even know George de Forest Brush, one of the teachers he lists on this form. In a letter from Proctor to Morris dated 19 April 1910 (AGO, Stone Bequest), following an earlier letter in which Proctor had proposed that Morris paint with Brush in Western Canada, Proctor writes, "I thought it would be a fine thing for you to know him ... I thought and still thought it would have been a good thing for you to have met Brush." This should not be taken that Morris had not ever studied with Brush; rather, that as a young student he had probably never impressed his personality on the older artist. Morris only became close to one of his teachers, William Cruikshank. Morris would later write a biography of Cruikshank, a copy of which is in the Morris "Invoice" book, p. 121. Across the top of it Morris wrote, "tackled the old man in his studio, drew this from him 26 May 1911."

8. EMM, *Early Diary,* 18 October 1894, p. 36: "Gérôme goes over my sketches and gives me a letter admitting me to the Beaux-Arts. I go to him occasionally

but seldom take criticisms.'' For a list of Canadians who went to Paris during these years, see *Canadians in Paris 1867-1914* (Art Gallery of Ontario, Toronto, 3 March — 15 April 1979), by David Wistow. This catalogue incorporates in an appendix the information compiled by Sylvain Allaire, "Les Canadiens au Salon officiel de Paris entre 1870 et 1910: Section Peintre et Dessin," *The Journal of Canadian Art History/Annales D'Histoire de L'Art Canadien*, IV, No. 2 (1977/78), 141-151.

9. Morris makes this observation about Gérôme in the same diary entry cited in n. 8; the list of the paintings, books and works of art he owned at the time of his death is in the AGO Archives.

10. EMM, *Early Diary*, 1897, pp. 48-49: "I go to Beaupré, Co. Montmorency, in a little village on the St. Lawrence three miles below St. Ann's — the Lourdes of Canada — and 23 below Quebec. No tourists and only a few Quebeckers. I find Dyonnet, Maurice Cullen here. I paint the habitants [p. 49] but they are extremely hard to get as models even when we pay them more than what they earn." He painted in this area for the next two summers. In an 1898 diary entry [p. 55], he notes that he, William Brymner and Cullen were staying together as they sketched; and the following year, a Toronto newspaper remarked that the three artists were again together ("Cullen, Brymner and Morris discontinue their sketching trip at Beaupré this week," *Saturday Night*, 21 October 1899, p. 9). These trips are also discussed by Sylvia Antoniou, in her catalogue *Maurice Cullen 1866-1934* (Agnes Etherington Arts Centre, Queen's University, Kingston, 26 September - 31 October 1982), esp. pp. 11-13. She identifies the hotel where the artists stayed together as Raymond's Hotel in Beaupré, and cites the article above from *Saturday Night* on p. 13, n. 86.

11. A recent exhibition discusses in some detail the popularity of this area of Quebec. See *Images de Charlevoix* (Musée des Beaux-Arts, Montreal, 27 November 1981 - 3 January 1982), cat. by Victoria Baker, esp. pp. 17-18. The Toronto-based artists who painted in this area include Lucius O'Brien, E. Wyly Grier, Charles O'Brien and F. M. Bell-Smith. Morris may therefore have been attracted to this area both because of his Quebec friends, and the many Toronto artists who came here. Morris knew Grier — he had shown him his sketches as early as 1893 (*Early Diary*, p. 21) — and Grier was a good friend of Edward Blake, the Toronto jurist, who had a summer home near La Malbaie.

12. Most of this information regarding Morris' exhibiting history comes from the Morris Letterbooks in the AGO, although in the back of this diary for 1886-1904 is an undated list of his early exhibitions, along with the names of the people who bought his paintings. All this information has been incorporated into an appendix, corroborated by other sources when possible.

13. Morris exhibited five paintings at the 1912 RCA exhibition. See Appendix A for a list of these.

14. EMM, *Early Diary* 1895, p. 42: "Working on *An Interior* [presumably *Spinning*] and *Girls in a Poppy Field*."

15. Interest in this school of painting has rekindled recently. See esp. *The Hague School. Dutch Masters of the 19th Century* (Royal Academy of Arts, London; London: Weidenfeld and Nicolson, 1983). See also Hermine G. Marius, *Dutch Painting in the Nineteenth Century*, trans. Alexander Teixeira de Mattos (London: De La More Press, 1908), rpt. as *Dutch Painters of the 19th Century*, ed. Geraldine Norman (Suffolk: Baron Publishing, 1973, 1983).

16. EMM, *Early Diary,* 12 December 1894 (although the page has 1895 written on it in Morris' hand), p. 37: "Exhibition at Art Club. Sent sketch of Iroquois. It was generally liked amongst the artists."

17. EMM, *Early Diary,* 1904, pp. 94-100, where he lists the exhibitions he had sent works to up to 1904. He lists two about which it has not been possible to find additional information, one held in Kilmarnock, Scotland in 1904, and one in Winnipeg that same year.

18. Scott had earlier made a similar trip, and described it in "The Last of the Indian Treaties." *Scribner's Magazine,* 40 (November 1906), pp. 573-583.

19. Scott's more than one hundred photographs of this trip are housed in the Ontario Archives, Toronto.

20. These photographs are in the Manitoba Archives, Winnipeg.

21. Morris recorded these trips in his *Western Diary.*

22. Edmund Morris to Premier Walter Scott, 2 September 1911, Manitoba Archives, Winnipeg.

23. This painting was exhibted with the CAC in 1912, cat. no. 52, with an illustration in the catalogue.

24. This opinion was expressed by J. D. Logan, in a pompous review of the CAC's 1912 exhibition titled, "Canadian Art Club Advances in Craftmanship and Vision," copy in the library of the National Gallery of Canada, Ottawa, vertical file on the CAC.

25. Lynne C. Doyle, "Art Notes," *Saturday Night,* 9, No. 16 (7 March 1896), 9.

26. Lynne C. Doyle, *Saturday Night,* 9, No. 49 (24 October 1896), 9.

27. "Studio Talk," *International Studio,* XII, No. 50 (April 1901), 209-210.

28. W. M. Boultbee, "Edmund Morris, Painter," *Canadian Magazine,* XXXI, No. 2 (May - October 1908), 121-127.

29. E. F. B. Johnston, "The Canadian Art Club, A Review of the Exhibition," *The Mail and Empire,* 8 February 1908, copy NGC, vertical file on the CAC.

30. "Canadian Art is given fresh stimulus," Toronto *World* 4 February 1908, p. 7f.

31. *Catalogue of Loan Collection of Objects of Indian Art and Curios on View at the Exhibition of Indian Portraits by Edmund Morris* (Canadian Art Club, Toronto, 30 March - 17 April 1909; Toronto: Miln-Bingham Printers, [1909]. An expanded version of the catalogue was also published, with ethnographic notes by Morris. See *Exhibition of Indian Portraits with notes on the tribes, by Edmund Morris* . . . (Toronto: Miln-Bingham Printers, 1909).

32. Byron E. Walker, as reported in the *News,* 30 March 1909, copy, Morris "Invoice" book, p. 27. Walker was a knowledgeable patron and important local collector, as well as being centrally important to the development of Canadian cultural institutions such as the National Gallery. For his activities as a collector, see Katharine A. Lochnan, "The Walker Journals: Reminiscences of John Lavery and William Holman Hunt," *RACAR: Revue d'art*

canadienne/Canadian Art Review, IX, Nos. 1/2 (1982), 57-63. See also *Sir Edmund Walker, Print Collector* (Art Gallery of Ontario, Toronto, 22 November 1974 - 12 January 1975), catalogue by Katharine Jordan [Lochnan], and *Images of Eighteenth-Century Japan. Ukiyoe Prints from the Sir Edmund Walker Collection* (Toronto: Royal Ontario Museum, 1975) by David Waterhouse.

33. *American Art News,* 24 April 1909, copy Manitoba Archives, Winnipeg.

34. Undated review, copy Morris "Invoice" book, p. 4.

35. James Mavor, "The Canadian Art Club," undated, copy NGC library, vertical file on the CAC, reprinted in *The Canadian Art Club,* 1907-1911, Edmund Morris, comp. (?) [Toronto, 1911], p. 21. Mavor was as important to the Toronto art world as Walker, albeit in a different way. He was active as a critic and author, in, for instance, *Notes on Appreciation of Art and on Art in Ontario* (Toronto: George N. Morang, [1898]), and in many other publications, including most of the early catalogues of the Art Museum of Toronto (now the Art Gallery of Ontario). For an introduction to Mavor, see *James Mavor and his World* (Thomas Fisher Rare Book Library, University of Toronto, June - July 1975).

36. "The Canadian Art Club Amanuensis," *Acta Victoriana,* XXXII, No. 6 (March 1909), 471, copy AGO library, Morris Scrapbooks, "Invoice" book, pp. 22-23, "An Art Exhibition," *The Canadian Courier,* 11 March 1911, p. 9, copy also in "Invoice" book, p. 93.

37. "The Canadian Art Club's Exhibition," *Saturday Night,* 11 March 1911, copy Morris "Invoice" book, pp. 98-99.

38. Logan's review is cited in note 24.

39. The quote ending with the word 'arrangement' is taken from the *Acta Victoriana,* as cited in note 36; the second copy comes from an anonymous review of the Club's 1912 exhibition, a copy of which is in the Morris "Invoice" book, p. 105.

40. Hector Charlesworth, "The Canadian Art Club, 1914," *Saturday Night,* copy Morris "Invoice" book, loose in folder.

41. Newton MacTavish, *The Fine Arts in Canada* (Toronto: The Macmillan Company of Canada, Limited, 1925), ch. viii, "The Canadian Art Club," pp. 69-74, esp. p. 71, where he writes, "Morris continued to be the energizing and binding force in the Club's activities."

42. Correspondence concerning preparations for this 1928 memorial exhibition is found in the AGO Archives. Morris left 119 paintings to the OCA to be sold to found a scholarship in his name (the scholarship still exists; it is worth approximately $100 annually). A list of paintings was prepared as early as 2 December 1913; a copy is attached to a letter dated 5 February 1918 from E. R. Greig, the Gallery's registrar, and William Morris, Edmund's brother. Matters dragged on for some years more before the sale was actually held in 1928.

43. An article in the *Toronto Telegram,* 21 June 1928, a copy of which is in the Morris artist's file in the AGO library, reads, "A shame. The prices paid for many charming paintings by Edmund M. Morris were small. 'In Camp' went for $5, 'Silver and Grey' for $5, 'Golden Harvest' for $5.50, 'Woodland' for $5,

'Autumn Evening' for the same, 'Landscape Inversary' [sic] for $14, 'Fishing Boat Low Tide' for $6.50, 'Dufferin Terrace, Quebec,' for $24, 'Story-Telling' for $3 and 'Low Tide, June', for $10. These were just a few.''

44. Reid, *A Concise History,* ch. ix, ''The Canadian Art Club,'' pp. 118-134.

45. Jean McGill, cited in note 1, has prepared a biography of Morris for publication; Mary Fitz-Gibbon, ROM research assistant, has prepared his 1907-1910 diary for publication and transcribed his earlier diaries for possible later publication.

46. Many Canadian artists of the late nineteenth century tried their hands at Indian portraits, with indifferent success. Frederick Verner (1836-1928) was still painting in the romantic illustrative vein of Paul Kane (1810-71). Typical of Verner's paintings of Indian subjects are his *Indian Encampment at Sunset* 1873 (Winnipeg Art Gallery, illustrated in Reid, *A Concise History,* p. 89), or *Indian Encampment on Georgian Bay* of 1866 (AGO).

Morris' close contemporary James Henderson (1871-1951) emigrated to Canada from Glasgow in 1909 and painted Indian portraits from about 1920. These show no advance on Morris' portraits. See *An Exhibition of Paintings by James Henderson, 1871-1851* (Mendel Art Gallery, Saskatoon, 1969), cat. 6, *Red Breath* (Sioux Portrait), c. 1920 (Prince Albert, p.c.) Other painters of Indians in Morris' generation inlcuded Augustus Kenderdine (1870-1947), who was born in Manchester, trained at Julian's in 1890-91 and emigrated to Lashburn, Saskatchewan in 1908; he painted Indian subjects after 1920; and John Innes (1863-1941), known for his 'Epic of Canada' series completed for the Hudson's Bay Company. Like Morris, Innis was a student of Cruikshank's, and was a member of the OSA in 1904, the year before Morris' election to the OSA.

See *Grandmaison, Henderson and Kenderdine: Painters of the Prairies* (Gordon Snelgrove Gallery, University of Saskatchewan, Saskatoon, 14 May - 6 June 1979), and John Bruce Cowan, *John Innes Painter of the Canadian West* (Vancouver: Rose, Cowan & Latta Limited, 1945).

A most unusual and early Indian painting which shows an excellent portrait quality is by William Brymner. *Giving Rations to the Blackfoot Indians, NWT* (Hamilton Art Gallery). It was executed in 1886, and is an evocative and sensitive portrait. See *William Brymner A Retrospective* (Agnes Etherington Arts Centre, Queen's University, Kingston, 13 May - 1 July 1979), catalogue by Janet Braide, cat. no. 16, illus. p. 81. Despite its accurate rendering of Indian physiognomy, however, Brymner's painting still evokes a feeling of pathos which makes it smack of genre painting. This differentiates it from Morris' unanectodal and non-sentimental portraits. Nonetheless, a painting such as Brymner's may well have shown Morris how forceful paintings of Indians could be.

47. John J. Bigsby, *The Shoe and Canoe, or Pictures of Travels in the Canadas,* 2 vols. (London: Chapman and Hall, 1850), I, plate facing p. 185.

48. EMM, *1906 Diary,* pp. 32 and 45.

49. EMM, *1906 Diary,* pp. 48 and 49.

50. A major exhibition on the Hague School in Europe has been cited in note 15; the extraordinary dominance of this school among Canadian collectors has long been recognized, but has only recently been examined in any detail. See *Collecting the Hague School in Canada* (Art Gallery of Ontario, Toronto, 7

May - 26 June 1983). This exhibition, organized by Marta Hurdalek, is still in circulation and a catalogue is expected.

51. It is a commonly-known irony in Canadian art history that the first art book published in Canada was on the Hague School, Montreal collector E. B. Greenshield's *Landscape Painting and Modern Dutch Artists,* published in 1906. Greenshield (1850 - 1918) was a Montreal dry-goods merchant.

52. In addition to Morris' diary entry cited in note 14, an article in *Saturday Night,* 7 March 1896, p. 7, notes that he had been sketching in Holland the previous summer. And he could well have known Hague School work before he ever went to Holland, since it was frequently exhibited in North-America. As early as 1892, when he was in New York, there had been an exhibition of Hague School work as part of the Columbia Exposition; Morris notes in his diary for 1892 that he has attended this exposition, and may well have seen the Hague School work, which was part of an exhibition titled *Exhibition by American Fine Arts Society of the Pictures Contributed by Sweden, Norway and Holland to the World's Columbia Exposition.* Moreover, there were frequent exhibitions of Hague School work in Montreal; the Art Association organized loan exhibitions annually from 1897 to 1900, and frequently thereafter. A list of these and other exhibitions which included Hague School work is given in *The Hague School,* Royal Academy, London, 1983, p. 322.

53. For this period in American art, see especially *American Art in the Barbizon Mood* (National Collection of Fine Arts, Smithsonian Institution, Washington, 23 January - 30 April 1975; Washington: Published for the National Collection of Fine Arts by the Smithsonian Institution Press, 1975), cat. by Peter Bermingham.

54. Duncan Campbell Scott, *The Poems of Duncan Campbell Scott* (Toronto: McClelland & Stewart, Publishers, Limited, 1926), pp. 141-150. For correspondence between Scott and his friend Pelham Edgar concerning this poem, see Leon Slonim, "A Critical Edition of the Poems of Duncan Campbell Scott," 2 vols. (Diss. University of Toronto, 1978), I, pp. 139-145, II, pp. 518-532.

55. He presumably met Morrice in Paris before 1897, since correspondence between them starts this year: see the Morrice artist's file in the AGO library. He probably met Cullen before 1895, since in a diary entry of this year he notes, "Cullen is elected an Associate this year" [of the Société Nationale des Beaux-Arts]. (EMM, *Early Diary,* 1895, p. 38.) Morris definitely met Horatio Walker in 1897, probably introduced to him by Montreal collector Charles Porteous. In a letter to Morris dated 17 October 1897, Byron Walker mentions that Porteous "tells me that you have met Horatio Walker, so I presume the number of painters had increased somewhat after you wrote. Porteous was enthusiastic about the work you were doing and he is not often enthusiastic about anything." This letter is in the AGO Stone Bequest. These meetings are confirmed by Sylvia Antoniou, *Maurice Cullen,* pp. 12-13.

56. EMM, *Early Diary,* 1893, p. 21: "I shall never forget Manet's *Boy with a Sword* — also some Romney portraits that I saw".

57. EMM, *Early Diary,* 1896, p. 47.

58. EMM, *Western Diary,* 22 July 1907, p. 11, p. 6, of t.s.

59. EMM, *Western Diary,* 26-29 July 1907, pp. 13-16, pp. 7-8 t.s.

60. EMM, *Western Diary,* 28 July 1907, p. 15, p. 8 t.s.

61. Edmund Morris, "The Indian Problem," *Winnipeg Free Press,* 25 October 1910, copy Manitoba Archives, Winnipeg.

62. His training in Europe and New York made Morris acutely aware of the inadequacies of art facilities in Toronto. On 19 January 1900, he wrote in his diary (p. 69), "the Normal School is a disgrace — will take steps to have a proper museum for the city." Morris did more than just complain. During his scant two years' membership in the OSA, he worked himself up to the managing committee for the OSA's annual exhibition (OSA, *Minute Books,* Ontario Archives, Toronto, 26 February 1907, p. 187). Morris then quickly joined his more progressive-minded painting colleagues in their decision in 1907 to found the Canadian Art Club, an alternative to the stodgy OSA. But he did not abandon the idea of working toward a museum for the city. See EMM, *Western Diary,* 1909, p. 90, p. 45 t.s.: "I have been appointed a member of the Council of the Toronto Art Museum — we have at last got a good gallery to make a start — and before leaving [for his third Western Journey], I called a meeting of our Canada Art Club and proposed we use the Museum for our annual Exhibitions instead of altering the Old Court House ...". A quote such as this is ample evidence of Morris' crucial importance in Club affairs. Morris was also a member of the Arts and Letters Club, joining in 1910, two years after its founding, according to Hunter Bishop, Arts and Letters Club archivist.

63. See the Edmund Morris Letterbooks. Compiling the Wyatt Eaton Scrapbooks occupied him intermittently from 1902 to 1911; and there are numerous instances in the Letterbooks which show his interest in the biographies of living Canadian artists.

64. Edmund Morris to Premier Walter Scott, 6 March 1911, Manitoba Archives, Winnipeg.

65. EMM, *Western Diary,* 1909, p. 155, p. 73 t.s.

66. Morris' letter to Walker has not been found, but on 5 February 1909, Walker has written Morris saying that he has received a telegram from Morris asking him to contact Proctor. This letter is in the Morris Letterbooks, I, p. 18.

67. Horatio Walker to Morris, 24 January (?) 1909, Morris Letterbooks, I, p. 20.

68. A. P. Proctor to Morris, 12 February 1909, Morris Letterbooks, I, p. 21-22.

69. Proctor to Morris, 25 April 1909, Stone Bequest, AGO.

70. Newton MacTavish, *Ars Longa* (Toronto: The Ontario Publishing Co., Limited, 1938), p. 166.

71. Proctor to Morris, 22 April 1913, Morris Letterbooks, I, p. 134.

72. Proctor to Morris, 29 April 1913, Morris Letterbooks, I, 136.

73. A. Jacacci to Morris, 6 May 1913, Morris Letterbooks, I, p. 141.

74. Each of these artists went on to exhibit with the Club. Correspondence between them and Morris is found in the Morris Letterbooks and in the Stone Bequest.

75. J. Kerr Lawson to Morris, 8 January 1912, Morris Letterbooks, I, p. 98.

76. Clarence Gagnon to Morris, 22 January 1910, Morris Letterbooks, I, p. 33.

77. Gagnon to Morris, 21 January 1913, Morris Letterbooks, I, p. 109.

78. Although it is equally clear that he thought any Toronto exhibition was a distant bet. In an often-quoted letter of 12 February 1911, Morrice writes Morris, "... I am becoming doubtful about the advisability of sending pictures to Toronto. Nothing is sold (except to our excellent friend MacTavish) — nobody understands them ... I have not the slightest desire to improve the taste of the Canadian public." This letter is in the Morrice artist's file, AGO library. But Morrice continued to send works for exhibit with the CAC; his sardonic tone was endemic.

79. Morrice to Morris, 5 April 1908, artist's file, AGO library: "In your last letter you said that this summer you intended going West to paint the red-skins, the Sioux Indians, and that you had done the same thing last year. Now I should like very much to go with you if it is agreeable to you. The change will be good for me and the prospect of painting something so entirely new is extremely fascinating." Morrice, apparently not having heard from Morris, writes again 26 April, asking him again about painting Indians, and urging him to "make a struggle and reply." Morrice apparently admired Morris' Indian portraits, for he suggested in a letter dated 26 May 1909 that Morris send four of his portraits to the Salon d'Automne in Paris; Morrice mentions the Indian portraits in another letter of 15 June 1909, when he realizes that since the portraits have all been purchased by the Ontario Government, they will probably not be available for exhibition. These letters are all in the Morrice artist's file, AGO library. The letter by Morrice to Morris dated 5 April 1908, and several others, are cited by John O'Brian, in "Morrice — O'Conor, Gauguin, Bonnard et Vuillard," *Dossier Art Canadien, Revue de l'Université de Moncton,* 15, Nos. 2/3 (avril - déc. 1982), 9-34, p. 21 and elsewhere.

80. Scott, *Poems of Duncan Campbell Scott,* 148. Scott took two years to write this poem, and incorporated several suggestions made by Pelham Edgar. The source of the correspondence between Scott and Edgar is cited in note 54.

Fig. 21   Edmund Morris, Kyaiyii and Chief
Nepahpenais 1909
Photo: Courtesy of Art Gallery of Ontario,
Toronto

46

EDMUND MORRIS:
THE GOVERNMENT OF SASKATCHEWAN PORTRAIT COMMISSION

Edmund Morris was born the year Paul Kane died. While Kane (1810 - 1871) was one of the first explorer-artists in Canada to record Indian types, he belonged to an era which perceived the noble savage through an entirely romantic and European sensibility. Nonetheless his avowed intent was to document a race of people before the demise of their culture as a result of European influence.[1] This sentiment was echoed by Edmund Morris a generation later in correspondence with Walter Scott, then Premier of Saskatchewan, regarding the commission of fifteen Indian portraits for the province:

> One point I wish to lay great stress on in connection with the work I propose doing for your government. The importance of losing no time as the last of the fighting Indians will soon be gone and then it will be impossible to get true records of the old type of those who held land before the coming of the whites.[2]

The importance of wasting no time was a hallmark of Edmund Morris' life and career as an artist. It was with dispatch that he carried out his initial commission for Indian portraits from the Ontario Government in 1906 on a journey to James Bay. Following the success of that venture, the Ontario Government further commissioned him to travel in Western Canada to record those Indians who had been involved in the treaty settlements. This he accomplished during the summers of 1907 and 1908, his first two Western Journeys. With a similar spirit of enterprise he left for his third trip to the West in July 1909 to contact personally the Governments of Saskatchewan and Alberta.

From his hotel in Regina, he wrote Walter Scott proposing "a series of twenty-five portraits representing the Indian tribes of Saskatchewan at $200 each within the next two years."[3] Scott was sympathetic to the idea, for Morris recorded in his diary a meeting later that evening with the Premier and "a long talk with him on art matters."[4] The following day Morris left Regina, arriving in Banff by the beginning of August. Here he met with A. C. Rutherford, Premier of Alberta, and received a commission for five portraits for the Legislative Building in Edmonton (see cats. 21 to 25).[5]

With this commission in hand, Morris received a letter shortly thereafter from Walter Scott authorizing him to proceed with a reduced number of fifteen portraits representing the Indian tribes of Saskatchewan at $200 each for delivery in late 1910.[6] At the same moment, Morris was writing to Scott with typical impatience:

> I am a litte uneasy as some of the best types are liable to shuffle off to the happy hunting grounds where they will be young again and have lots of horses and buffalos![7]

A month later, Morris returned to Toronto where he immersed himself over the winter with organizational details for the Canadian Art Club. He resumed his correspondence with Walter Scott in the spring of 1910 to inform him that he had finished a portrait of

Fig. 22 *Indian Tepees,* Photograph by
Edmund Morris
Manitoba Archives, Winnipeg

Fig. 23 Edmund Morris, *Indian Tepees:
Manitoba,* c. 1911
(cat. 37)

48

Chief Poundmaker for the Saskatchewan Government (cat. 34). Although Poundmaker had died in 1886, Morris stated "As he is counted one of the finest types the Red race has produced, I thought it necessary to include him."[8] This was the first work to reach Regina before Morris' arrival in late July 1910 during his fourth Western Journey. He recorded in his diary:

> About the 25th I go to Regina to hand over five of the portraits to the Govt. Hon. Mr. Scott & his ministers come to the King's Hotel to see them & are much pleased with the result (the Deputy Minister & the Minister of Education.[9]

Fig. 24 *Big Darkness (Opazatonka)*
Photograph by Edmund Morris, c. 1910
Manitoba Archives, Winnipeg

Fig. 25 Edmund Morris, *Big Darkness (Opazatonka)*, 1910
(cat. 27)

Fig. 27   Edmund Morris, *High Eagle
(Pitauspitau),* 1909
(cat. 25)

Fig. 26   *High Eagle (Pitauspitau)*
Photograph by Edmund Morris, c. 1909
Manitoba Archives, Winnipeg

Morris spent the rest of the summer of 1910 working on the commission, travelling to
Indian reserves in Saskatchewan. Before returning to the East, he stopped at Regina in
September to look at the first works hanging temporarily in Government House before
the opening of the new Legislative Building.[10] By March 1911, the second shipment of
five works had arrived and were hung in advance of the opening of the assembly
chamber in the offices of the Minister of Education and the Deputy Minister of Public
Works. A Deputy Minister was so enthusiastic about the works that he wrote to
Morris: "I do not claim to be a critic myself, but as far as I am aware, they are A. No. 1
variety."[11]

Morris hoped that the positive response generated by these works and the last shipment
which arrived before 1 September 1911 would stir Scott and his Government to
consider a further commission for "groups of the Indian lodges in the surrounding
landscape. There are still many of the painted lodges with designs of the thunder bird
they worship. These with a suggestion of Indian life about them make fine subjects for
painting."[12] (figs. 22 - 23). While a further commission was not forthcoming, Morris
must have felt satisfaction that a significant number of his portraits would be
permanently lodged in the new Saskatchewan Legislative Building.

Edmund Morris was an artist with a mission. But this should not disguise the fact that he was first and foremost an artist rather than an ethnographer. Although Morris sought and justified commissions from the provincial governments on the basis of his works' lasting historical significance, it was the artistic potential of the Indian portraits which motivated the work. That Morris exhibited them with the Canadian Art Club is witness to his desire to establish an artistic reputation equal to that of his colleagues. Following his 1909 one-man exhibition of fifty-five portraits in Toronto, some writers were quick to seize upon the merits of the work. One critic for *Saturday Night* noted:

> There are paintings which are interesting as works of art, and others whose interest lies in their subject. The pictures recently exhibited in the Canadian Art Gallery by Mr. Edmund Morris possess both claims on public attention. They are a series of portraits of the most prominent living redmen in Canada, and both as pieces of portraiture and as the finest possible souvenirs of a race which will soon be no more than a tradition, they deserve every consideration.[13]

Fig. 28   *Chief Water Chief (Okena)*
Photograph by Edmund Morris, c. 1909
Manitoba Archives, Winnipeg

Fig. 29   Edmund Morris, *Chief Water Chief (Okena),* 1909
(cat. 23)

While the biographies and anecdotes gathered by Morris in his *Western Diary* provide a fascinating account of his subects, it is the portraits which best reveal him as a sympathetic observer of the native people.[14] Morris wanted to portray the individual, not a stereotype. From photographs taken by the artist of his subjects, it is clear how faithful he was to appearance (see figs. 24 - 35). These photographs were never slavishly copied, but rather acted as a record for consultation by Morris if further work on costume or finishing touches were required after the sitting. Generally however, Morris' method was to establish the principal facial characteristics and compositional elements in the field, thereby imparting a sense of immediacy to the work (see figs. 7 - 8).

Fig. 31   Edmund Morris, *Chief Spring Chief (Ninau Ksis Kum),* 1909
(cat. 21)

Fig. 30   Cropped view of *Chief Spring Chief (Ninau Ksis Kum)*
Photograph by Edmund Morris, c. 1909
Manitoba Archives, Winnipeg

Fig. 32 *Black Eagle (Sixsipita)*
Photograph by Edmund Morris, c. 1907
Manitoba Archives, Winnipeg

Fig. 33 Edmund Morris, *Black Eagle (Sixsipita),*
1907
(cat. 18)

By the time Morris executed the works for the Saskatchewan commission in 1910, he was at the height of his powers as a portrait painter. Whereas his first efforts for the Ontario Government at James Bay in 1906 concentrated exclusively on the head, his later work encompassed the entire sheet of paper allowing details of costume to contribute a significant role. A particularly handsome example is *Pahnap, Medicine Man* (cat. 30). Another work, *Moses* (cat. 28), is a powerful evocation of the character of the sitter expressed through his direct gaze at the viewer. The skillful modelling of the face with judiciously placed highlights underscores Morris' facility with pastel, a difficult medium to handle due to the risk of its smudging.

Morris' favourite subject may well have been *Nepahpenais — Night Bird,* a Saskatchewan chief he knew by 1909 (fig. 21), and portrayed at least five times.[15] In his diary, Morris recorded the exploits of the chief which he learned in conversation during the portrait sitting.[16] That Morris captured the essential likeness of his subject is clear from a comparison with a contemporary photograph (fig. 35). Three years later in 1913, *Nepahpenais* was portrayed by the English expatriate artist Inglis Sheldon-Williams (1870 - 1940) who had just returned to Canada that year.

Fig. 34   Edmund Morris, *Nepahpenais — Night Bird,* 1910 (cat. 31)

Fig. 36   Inglis Sheldon-Williams (1870 - 1940) *Chief Nepahpenais — Night Bird,* 1913 watercolour on cardboard 10¾ × 8¾ (27.3 × 22.2) Norman Mackenzie Art Gallery, Regina

Fig. 35 *Nepahpenais — Night Bird*
Photograph by Edmund Morris, c. 1910
Manitoba Archives, Winnipeg

Fig. 37   James Henderson (1871 - 1951)
Mato-e-yanke, A Sioux Indian (before 1924)
oil on canvas, 30 × 24 (76.2 × 61.0)
Norman Mackenzie Art Gallery, Regina
Gift of Mr. Norman Mackenzie

Fig. 38   Augustus Kenderdine (1870 - 1947)
Study of a Cree Indian
watercolor, pencil and chalk on paper
24 × 173/16 × (61.0 × 43.7)
Norman Mackenzie Art Gallery

While Morris' portraits of Saskatchewan Indians in the Legislative Building in Regina from 1912 may have been an inspiration to Sheldon-Williams, they also paved the way for future Indian portrait painters in Saskatchewan such as James Henderson (1871 -1951) and Augustus Kenderdine (1870 - 1947). Although contemporaries, Henderson and Kenderdine painted Indian subjects some years later than Morris in a more romantic and less individual way (figs. 37 - 38). By the twenties, Morris' fears regarding the imminent disappearance of the last "Indian who went on the warpath and hunted the buffalo" had come all too true. It is due to the foresight of Walter Scott and his Government's commission to Edmund Morris that Saskatchewan has not only a lasting historical record of importance for the province, but also a collection of works which rank among the finest Indian portraits in the history of Canadian art.

Michael Parke-Taylor

NOTES

1. For a useful discussion of Paul Kane and George Catlin (1796 - 1872) as predecessors to Morris, see Ann Davis, "Indians' Historians: George Catlin and Paul Kane", *A Distant Harmony* (Winnipeg Art Gallery, 8 October - 28 November 1982), pp. 33-68. Morris expressed the view that "In reality Paul Kane was an adventurer & explorer but his works have a value and in craftsmanship they are better than the other Indian painter, Catlin." EMM, *Western Diary,* 8 October 1909, p. 145, p. 68 t.s.

2. Edmund Morris to Walter Scott, 21 July 1909, microfilm Saskatchewan Archives, Regina.

3. Morris to Scott, 20 July 1909, Manitoba Archives, Winnipeg.

4. EMM, *Western Diary,* [20 July 1909], p. 92, p. 45 t.s.

   Ever a promoter of his CAC colleagues, Morris continued by suggesting that the Government of Saskatchewan commission the sculptor A. P. Proctor to make statues of buffalo for either side of the entrance of the proposed Legislative Building and for the prison. These projects were never realized.

5. See EMM, *Western Diary,* [Aug. 1909], pp. 93-94, p. 46 t.s.

   The completed series of five portraits for which the government paid $200 each, were received by the Government of Alberta 30 May 1910. The entire commission is included in this exhibition (cats. 21 - 25).

6. Scott to Morris, 2 September 1909, Manitoba Archives, Winnipeg. In a follow-up letter dated 7 September 1909 (Manitoba Archives, Winnipeg), Scott proposed "that five be delivered on or before the 1st September 1910, the second five on or before the 1st March 1911, and the remaining five on or before 1st September 1911."

7. Morris to Scott, 2 September 1909, Manitoba Archives, Winnipeg.

8. Morris to Scott, 25 May 1910, microfilm Saskatchewan Archives, Regina. Morris must have executed this portrait from a photograph as *Poundmaker* died in 1886. A work related to the portrait in the Saskatchewan Government Collection is in the collection of the Department of Ethnology, Royal Ontario Museum.

9. EMM, *Western Diary,* [after 25th July 1910], pp. 212, p. 101 t.s.

10. Morris to Scott, 17 October 1910, microfilm Saskatchewan Archives, Regina. In this letter, Morris proposed that the works be hung in the billiard room. He thought the light there was better than in the rest of the building.

11. Deputy Minister, Government of Saskatchewan, to Morris, 10 April 1911, Manitoba Archives, Winnipeg.

12. Morris to Scott, 2 September 1911, microfilm Saskatchewan Archives, Regina.

13. "A Painter of Indians", *Saturday Night,* 24 April 1909, vol. 22, p. 2.

14. Morris also provided biographical details on the following Indians from the Saskatchewan commission: Nepahpenais, Night Bird; Acoose, "Man Standing Above Ground"; Walter Ochopowace; Kakakapechamaskis, "The Man Who Ties The Knot"; Pimotat; Chagakin, "Chief Carry the Kettle"; Big Darkness, Opazatonka; in his "Portraits of the Aborigines of Canada and Notes on the Tribes", *Catalogue of the Morris Collection of Indian Portraits At the Gallery of the Canadian Art Club,* 1909. For further biographical descriptions of Indians in the Saskatchewan commission, see *Catalogue of Historical Paintings*

in the Legislative Building, Regina, Saskatchewan. Issued by authority of Hon. J. F. Bryan, Minister of Public Works, 1933 (Saskatchewan Archives, Regina). Jean McGill noted where the Indians lived in Saskatchewan in "Edmund Morris Among the Saskatchewan Indians and the Fort Qu'Appelle Monument", *Saskatchewan History* XXXV, No. 3 (Autumn 1982), 107.

15. Other Morris portraits of *Nepahpenais* may be identified in the collection of the Department of Ethnology, Royal Ontario Museum; The Winnipeg Art Gallery, the Glenbow Museum, and one was sold at Christie's, Montreal, 8 May 1975, lot 27.

16. EMM, *Western Diary,* July 1910, p. 202, t.s. 97.

EDMUND MORRIS: THE GOVERNMENT OF SASKATCHEWAN PORTRAIT COMMISSION

1. *Big Darkness (Opazatonka),*
   pastel on paper
   25³/₁₆ × 19¾ (63.9 × 50.1)
   Signed l.r.: *Edmund Morris*

2. *Moses,*
   pastel on paper
   25³/₁₆ × 19¾ (63.9 × 50.1)
   Signed l.r.: *Edmund Morris*

3. *Chief Nepahpenais — Night Bird*, 1910
   pastel on paper
   25 3/16 × 19¾ (63.9 × 50.1)
   Signed l.l.: *Edmund Morris 1910*

4. *The Walker (Pimotat)*
   pastel on paper
   25 3/16 × 19¾ (63.9 × 50.1)
   Signed l.r.: *Edmund Morris*

5. *Walter Ochopowace*
   pastel on paper
   25 3/16 × 19¾ (63.9 × 50.1)
   Signed l.r.: *Edmund Morris*

6. *Chief Poundmaker (Pee-Too-Kah-Han)*
   pastel on paper
   25 3/16 × 19¾ (63.9 × 50.1)
   Signed l.r.: *Edmund Morris*

7

8

9

7. *Thunder Bear (Peeaysen Musquah) called Shee Sheep — Little Duck*
   pastel on paper
   25³/₁₆ × 19¾ (63.9 × 50.1)
   Signed l.l.: *Edmund Morris*

8. *Pahnap Medicine Man*
   pastel on paper
   25³/₁₆ × 19¾ (63.9 × 50.1)
   Signed l.r.: *Edmund Morris*

9. *Acoose, "Man Standing Above Ground"*
   pastel on paper
   25³/₁₆ × 19¾ (63.9 × 50.1)
   Signed l.r.: *Edmund Morris Acoose — Saulteaux*

10

11

12

10. *The Runner — Brother of Chief "Carry the Kettle"*, 1910
    pastel on paper
    25 3/16 × 19¾ (63.9 × 50.1)
    Signed l.l.: *Edmund Morris*

11. *Chagakin, "Carry the Kettle"*, 1910
    pastel on paper
    25 3/16 × 19¾ (63.9 × 50.1)
    Signed l.r.: *Edmund Morris*, 1910

12. *Mistahah Musqua, "Big Bear"*
    pastel on paper
    25 3/16 × 19¾ (63.9 × 50.1)
    Signed l.r.: Boxed monogram of artist

13

14

15

13. *Kahtokopechamakasis, "The Man Who Ties The Knot,* 1910
    pastel on paper
    23 3/16 × 19¾ (63.9 × 50.1)
    Signed l.l.: *Edmund Morris*

14. *Piapot,* 1910
    pastel on paper
    25 3/16 × 19¾ (63.9 × 50.1)
    Signed l.r.: Boxed monogram of artist

15. *Ometaway, "Gambler",* 1910
    pastel on paper
    25 3/16 × 19¾ (63.9 × 50.1)
    Signed l.l.: *Edmund Morris,* 1910

All works Collection of the Government of Saskatchewan, Regina

WORKS IN EXHIBITION

Measurements in inches and (centimeters); height precedes width

1. *Girls in a Poppy Field,* 1895
   oil on canvas
   27¼ × 22¼ (70.5 × 56.2)
   Signed l.r.: *E. M. Morris*
   Art Gallery of Ontario, Toronto
   Gift of Sir Edmund Walker, 1918

2. *Old Fort, Toronto,* c. 1890
   pencil
   7½ × 14½ (19.1 × 36.8)
   Signed l.r.: *Old Fort, Toronto*
   The Royal Ontario Museum, Toronto

3. *The Old Fort Toronto,* 1890
   sepia wash drawing
   7¾ × 11 1/8 (19.7 × 28.3)
   Signed l.l.: *The Old Fort, Toronto looking East E. Morris*
   The Women's Canadian Historical Society of Toronto

4. *A Block House, Fort York,* 1890
   pencil
   7 × 9 (17.8 × 22.9)
   Signed l.l.: *E. M. Morris Sept. 20, 1890*
   The Royal Ontario Museum, Toronto

5. *Old Fort, Toronto*, 1890
brown wash over pencil
9 × 12 (22.9 × 30.5)
Signed: l.r.: *E. M. Morris, April 24, 1890 The Old Fort*
The Royal Ontario Museum, Toronto

6. *The Old Fort, Toronto Looking West,* c. 1890
sepia wash drawing
7¾ × 11 3/16 (19.7 × 28.4)
Signed l.l.: *The Old Fort Toronto looking west E. Morris*
The Metropolitan Toronto Library, TII634

7. *Ship near Quebec,* c. 1896
   oil on panel
   4¼ × 6 (10.8 × 15.2)
   Unsigned
   William K. Schwarz and Nancy Schwarz, Cambridge

8. *Old Barn near Cap Tourmente,* c. 1896
   oil on panel
   4¼ × 6 (10.8 × 15.2)
   Unsigned
   William K. Schwarz and Nancy Schwarz, Cambridge

9. *Landscape near Quebec,* c. 1896
   oil on panel
   4¼ × 6 (10.8 × 15.2)
   Unsigned
   William K. Schwarz and Nancy Schwarz, Cambridge

10. *Landscape near Quebec,* c. 1896
    oil on panel
    4¼ × 6 (10.8 × 15.2)
    Unsigned
    William K. Schwarz and Nancy Schwarz, Cambridge

11. *Portrait of a Habitant,*
   pastel on paper
   14 × 10 (35.6 × 25.4)
   Signed u.r.: *E. Morris*
   Joan and W. Ross Murray, Whitby

12. *Cap Tourmente,* c. 1903
    oil on canvas
    23½ × 29½ (59.7 × 74.9)
    Signed l.l.: *Edmund Morris*
    National Gallery of Canada, Ottawa

13. *Last Light*
    oil on canvas
    $24 \times 30\frac{1}{8}$ (61.0 $\times$ 76.5)
    Signed l.l.: *Edmund M. Morris*
    Art Gallery of Hamilton
    Gift of Roy G. Cole, Esq. 1961

14. *Cove Fields, Quebec,* c. 1905
    oil on canvas
    29¾ × 40 (75.6 × 101.6)
    Signed l.r.: *Edmund Morris*
    National Gallery of Canada, Ottawa
    Gift of Alexander C. Morris, Toronto 1928

15. *Old Fort Edmonton,* c. 1910
    oil on canvas
    29½ × 40 (74.9 × 101.6)
    Signed l.l.: *Edmund Morris*
    Glenbow Museum, Calgary

16. *Indians Descending the Pic River,* 1906
    pastel on paper
    23½ × 23½ (59.7 × 59.7)
    Signed l.l.: *Edmund Morris Pic River 1906*
    Mr. C. R. Osler, Toronto

17. *A Northern River,* 1906
    oil on canvas
    29½ × 39 (74.9 × 99.0)
    Signed l.l.: *Edmund Morris*
    Government of Ontario Art Collection, Queen's Park, Toronto

18. *Black Eagle (Sixsipita),* 1907
pastel on paper
30 × 26 (76.2 × 66.0)
Signed u.r.: *Edmund Morris 1907*
Harold Groves, King City

19. *Chief Bull Plume (Stumiksisapo),* 1907
pastel on paper
25 × 19½ (63.5 × 49.5)
Signed l.l.: *Edmund Morris Piegan Reserve 1907*
Art Gallery of Ontario, Toronto
Bequest of Edmund Morris, 1922

20. *Portrait of an Indian*
    pastel on paper
    14 × 21 (35.6 × 53.3)
    Unsigned
    Harold Groves, King City

21. *Chief Spring Chief (Ninau Ksis Kum),* 1909
pastel on paper
25 3/16 × 19 11/16 (63.9 × 50.0)
Signed l.r.: *Edmund Morris 1909*
The Government of Alberta, Edmonton

22. *Wolf Collar (Makoyo Ki Na Si) Medicine Man,* 1909
pastel on paper
25 3/16 × 19 11/16 (63.9 × 50.0)
Signed l.l.: *Edmund Morris 1909*
The Government of Alberta, Edmonton

23. *Chief Water Chief (Okena),* 1909
pastel on paper
25 3/16 × 19¾ (63.9 × 50.2)
Signed l.r.: *Edmund Morris 1909*
The Government of Alberta, Edmonton

24. *White Buffalo Calf (Child-Unistaipoka),* 1909
pastel on paper
25 3/16 × 19¾ (63.9 × 50.1)
Signed l.r.: *Edmund Morris Kyai'yo 1909*
The Government of Alberta, Edmonton

25. *High Eagle (Pitauspitau),* 1909
pastel on paper
25¾ × 19⅝ (64.0 × 49.8)
Signed l.r.: *Edmund Morris Kyai'yo 1909*
The Government of Alberta, Edmonton

26. *Chief Star Blanket (Ahchukakopetokopit),* 1910
pastel on paper
$25_{1/8} \times 19_{11/16}$ (63.8 × 50.0)
Signed l.l.: *Edmund Morris 1910*
Norman Mackenzie Art Gallery, Regina
(Colour reproduction p. 8)

27. *Big Darkness (Opazatonka),* c. 1910
pastel on paper
25³/₁₆ × 19¾ (63.9 × 50.1)
Signed l.r.: *Edmund Morris*
The Government of Saskatchewan, Regina

28. *Moses,* c. 1910
pastel on paper
25³/₁₆ × 19¾ (63.9 × 50.1)
Signed l.r.: *Edmund Morris*
The Government of Saskatchewan, Regina
(Colour reproduction on cover)

29. *Thunder Bear (Peeaysen Musquah) called Shee Sheep — Little Duck,* c. 1910
pastel on paper
25³/₁₆ × 19¾ (63.9 × 50.1)
Signed l.l.: *Edmund Morris*
The Government of Saskatchewan, Regina

30. *Pahnap Medicine Man,* c. 1910
    pastel on paper
    25³/₁₆ × 19¾ (63.9 × 50.1)
    Signed l.r.: *Edmund Morris*
    The Government of Saskatchewan, Regina

31. *Chief Nepahpenais — Night Bird,* 1910
    pastel on paper
    25 3/16 × 19¾ (63.9 × 50.1)
    Signed l.l.: *Edmund Morris 1910*
    The Government of Saskatchewan, Regina

32. *The Walker (Pimotat),* c. 1910
pastel on paper
25³/₁₆ × 19¾ (63.9 × 50.1)
Signed l.r.: *Edmund Morris*
The Government of Saskatchewan, Regina

33. *Walter Ochopowace,* c. 1910
    pastel on paper
    25³/₁₆ × 19¾ (63.9 × 50.1)
    Signed l.r.: *Edmund Morris*
    The Government of Saskatchewan, Regina

34. *Chief Poundmaker (Pee-Too-Kah-Han),* c. 1910
pastel on paper
25³/₁₆ × 19¾ (63.9 × 50.1)
Signed l.r.: *Edmund Morris*
The Government of Saskatchewan, Regina

35. *Plains Indian on Horseback on a Bluff Overlooking a Plain,* c. 1909
oil on canvas
24 × 30 (60.9 × 76.2)
Signed l.r.: *Edmund Morris*
Harold Groves, King City

36. *Indian Encampment on the Prairie,* c. 1911
   oil on canvas
   24 × 30 (61.0 × 76.2)
   Signed l.l.: *Edmund Morris*
   Art Gallery of Ontario, Toronto
   Gift of Ontario College of Art, 1932

37. *Indian Tepees: Manitoba,* c. 1911
    oil on panel
    4¼ × 6 (10.8 × 15.2)
    Unsigned
    Provincial Archives of Manitoba, Winnipeg

38. *Sketch of Tepees,* c. 1911
    oil on panel
    4½ × 6 (11.4 × 15.2)
    Unsigned
    Harold Groves, King City

39. *Sketch of Tepees,* c. 1911
   oil on panel
   4½ × 6 (11.4 × 15.2)
   Unsigned
   Harold Groves, King City

CHRONOLOGY

1871
Born at Perth, Ontario 18 December 1871, to the Hon. Alexander Morris and Margaret Clive Morris.

1872 - 77
Edmund's father, the Hon. Alexander Morris holds post of Lieutenant-Governor of Manitoba and the Northwest Territories. Family moves to Fort Garry, [Winnipeg] Manitoba.

1877
Morris family moves to Toronto where Alexander Morris serves as member of the provincial legislature 1878 - 1886.

1888
Six-month apprenticeship with Toronto architect Frank Darling, starting January.

1889
Abandons architecture and on 2 October enters studio of William Cruikshank and sketches evenings at Art Students League, Toronto.

Death of father 28 October 1889.

1891
September: Goes to New York where he studies at Art Students League under Kenyon Cox, William Merritt Chase, Henry Siddons Mowbray and George de Forest Brush.

1892
Summer: Sketching near Toronto at Weston, the Humber River, Toronto Island, and Old Fort York.

Returns to New York in the fall where he attended the Columbia exposition and may have seen an Exhibition by the American Fine Arts Society of the Pictures contributed by Sweden, Norway, and Holland to the World's Columbia Exposition.

1893
October: Leaves via Montreal for studies in Paris at Académie Julian in the atélier of Jean-Paul Laurens and Benjamin Constant.

Attends Académie des Beaux Arts under Jean-Léon Gérôme.

1894
Spends summer in Scotland. Returns to Paris in fall.

1895
Summer: Sketching in Holland and Belgium.

1896
Spring: Returns to Toronto
Paints near Ste. Anne de Beaupré in Montmorency, Quebec with Maurice Cullen, William Brymner and Edmond Dyonnet.

1897

Summer: Paints at Beaupré with Brymner, Cullen and Dyonnet. Meets Horatio Walker probably through Montreal collector Charles Porteous.

1898

Elected Associate of the Royal Canadian Academy (A.R.C.A.) 4 March 1898.

July-August: Paints with Brymner, Cullen and Dyonnet at Louisbourg in the Lower St. Lawrence, in Ste. Anne Falls, St. Fériol and Beaupré.

1899

August-October: Paints with Brymner and Cullen at Beaupré and Baie St. Paul.

1900

Sketches near Ste. Anne's and Cap Tourmente, Quebec during the summer.

1901

Exhibits at Pan-American Exposition, Buffalo and is awarded bronze medal for *Girls in a Poppy Field*.

1902

Trip to Scotland and Holland where he paints numerous landscapes.

1903

Summer: Painting at Beaupré with Cullen and J. W. Morrice.

1904

Member of Women's Canadian Historical Society, Toronto.

1905

Elected member of the Ontario Society of Artists.

1906

Commissioned by Ontario Government to paint Ojibway in northern Ontario.

July-August: Accompanies Treaty Expedition Nine to James Bay.

September: Returns to Toronto having remained longer than treaty party to execute portraits.

1907

Resigns membership from OSA. Founding member of Canadian Art Club.

Further commission by the Ontario Government to paint portraits of Plains Indians for Parliament Buildings, Toronto.

28 June-mid October: First Western Journey. Travels from Toronto as far as British Columbia. Visits Indian reserves in Alberta near Calgary.

1908

26 June-October: Second Western Journey. Visits Indian reserves in Manitoba, Saskatchewan, and Alberta.

1909

Appointed member of Council of Toronto Art Museum.

30 March - 17 April: One-man exhibition of Indian portraits and Indian artifacts at Canadian Art Club, Old Court House, 57 Adelaide St. E., Toronto. In conjunction with the exhibition publishes *Catalogue of the Morris Collection of Indian Portraits with notes on the Tribes by Edmund Morris, Together with loan Collections of Indian Art and Curios, at the Gallery of the Club.* Toronto: Miln-Bingham, Printers, 1909.

July-October: Third Western Journey. Visits Manitoba and Saskatchewan where he tours Indian reservations to find subjects for portraits. Spends most of summer in Alberta at Indian reservations near Gleichen.

Commissioned by Government of Alberta to execute five Indian portraits for Legislative Building, Edmonton.

Commissioned by Government of Saskatchewan to execute fifteen Indian portraits for planned Legislative Building in Regina.

1910

Member of Arts and Letters Club, Toronto.

May: Completed series of five portraits for Government of Alberta.

16 June-October: Fourth Western Journey. Spends most of summer painting Indians in Saskatchewan. On 25 July Government of Saskatchewan receives first five commissioned portaits.

1911

March: Sends second installment of five portraits to Government of Saskatchewan.

August: Government of Saskatchewan receives final five portraits.

September: Paints portraits and Indian tepees in Saskatchewan.

Publishes work on Canadian artists: *Art in Canada: The Early Painters* [Toronto, 1911].

1912

February: Listed as Honorary Secretary for CAC in Canadian Art Club, 5th Annual, exhibition catalogue.

1913

Dies 21 August 1913 by drowning in St. Lawrence River during sketching outing while visiting Horatio Walker near Port Neuf, Quebec.

Buried 27 August 1913 Mount Pleasant Cemetery, Toronto.

1928

3 March-8 April: *Edmund Morris Memorial Exhibition,* Art Gallery of Toronto.

SELECTED BIBLIOGRAPHY

I. *Manuscript Sources*

Kingston. Queen's University. Archives. Collection 2140. *Edmund Morris Diaries, 1886 - 1904.* [Copy Ethnology Department, Royal Ontario Museum, Toronto]

_____. *Edmund Morris Diary of 1906. Treaty 9. Journey to James Bay.* [Copy Ethnology Department, Royal Ontario Museum, Toronto, ts. transcription by Mary Fitz-Gibbon]

North York. Public Library. The Canadiana Collection. *Newton MacTavish Collection.*

Ottawa. National Gallery of Canada. Reference Library. *Edmund Morris Vertical File.*

_____. Canadian Art Club Vertical File.

Ottawa. Public Archives of Canada. Manuscript Division. *Newton MacTavish Papers.* MG D278 vols. 3 and 4.

_____. [History of the Morris Family]. ts., by Edmund Morris (?). c. 1911. MG 30 D6.

_____. *Royal Canadian Academy Minute Books.* MG I 126 vol. 17.

_____. *Duncan Campbell Scott Papers.* MG 30 D100 vol. 3

Toronto. Art Gallery of Ontario. Reference Library. *Edmund Morris Letterbooks. Canadian Art Club Scrapbooks.*

_____. *Edmund Morris Artist's File.*

_____. *James Wilson Morrice Artist's File.* [27 letters to Morris, 1897 - 1911].

_____. *Homer Watson's Artists' File.*

Toronto. Ontario Archives. *Morris Family Papers.* Ms. 535.

_____. *Ontario Society of Artists' Minute Books, 1901 - 1915.* Ser. III, MU 2254, vol. VII.

_____. *Exhibition Catalogues, 1883 - 1944.* MU 3380.

_____. *Correspondence.* MU 2250.

_____. *Newspaper Clippings.* MU 2267.

_____. Picture Division. *Duncan Campbell Scott Collection.* [Photographs of 1906 Treaty Expedition to James Bay]

Toronto. Royal Ontario Museum. Ethnology Collections. *Transcription of Morris List of Picture Owners, Displays and Prices from Account Book.* ts., n.d., n.p.

_____. *Morris Account Book* [List of works sold 1897 - 1912]

_____. *Edmund Morris: Western Diary, 1907 - 1910.* [Ethnology Department, Royal Ontario Museum, Toronto, transcription by Mary Fitz-Gibbon.

Toronto. Victoria University. Library. *Pelham Edgar Papers.*

_____. *Duncan Campbell Scott Papers in the Pelham Edgar Papers.* Folders 36 - 46, correspondence, 1890 - 1946.

Toronto. University of Toronto. Thomas Fisher Rare Book Library. Ms. collection 13. *Duncan Campbell Scott Papers.*

_____. Ms. collection 119. *James Mavor Papers.*

_____. Ms. collection 1. *Sir Edmund Walker Papers.*

Winnipeg. Provincial Archives of Manitoba. *Edmund Morris Correspondence 1889 - 1913.*

_____. Still Images Section. *Edmund Morris Collection.* [Photographs by Edmund Morris c. 1907 - 1911]

II. (a)   *Writings by Edmund Morris*

Morris, Edmund. "Old Lords of The Soil. Description of Indians Living Near James Bay." *The News.* 9 May 1907.

Catalogue of Loan Collections of Objects of Indian Art and Curios on View at the Exhibition of Indian Portraits by Edmund Morris. (Toronto, Canadian Art Club, 57 Adelaide St. E., 30 March   17 April 1909.) Toronto: Miln-Bingham, Printers, [1909]. 12 p., no ills.

Catalogue of the Morris Collection of Indian Portraits at the Gallery of the Canadian Art Club. (Toronto, the Canadian Art Club, 29 March — 17 April 1909.) Toronto: Miln-Bingham Printers, [1909]. 22 p., 11 ills.

_____. "The Indian Problem." *Winnipeg Free Press.* 25 Oct. 1910.

_____. "An Ancient Indian Fort." *The Canadian Magazine of Politics, Science Art and Literature,* XXXVI (November 1910 to April 1911; Toronto: The Ontario Publishing Co., Limited 1911), pp. 257 - 259.

_____. "Art in Canada: The Early Painters." *Saturday Night.* 24, No. 15 (24 Jan. 1911), 25 and 29.

_____. *Art in Canada: The Early Painters.* [Toronto]: n.p., 1911.

_____. "Early Canadian Painters." *The Lamps.* The Arts and Letters Club, Toronto. 1, No. 2 (Dec. 1911), 8.

_____. comp. *Art in England.* [scrapbook, AGO Reference Library].

_____. comp. *Canadian Painters.* [scrapbook, AGO Reference Library].

_____. Wyatt Eaton Scrapbook. 2 vols. [AGO Reference Library.]

(b) *Chronological listing of newspaper references, reviews and articles, exclusively about Morris. Publications are from Toronto unless otherwise noted.*

Doyle, Lynne C. "Art Notes." *Saturday Night.* 9, No. 48 (17 October 1896), 9.

_____. [Review of Edmund Morris exhibition] *Saturday Night,* 9, No. 49 (24 October 1896), 9.

_____. "Art Notes." *Saturday Night,* 9, No. 16 (7 March 1896), 9.

_____. [Review of Edmund Morris exhibition] *Saturday Night,* 10, No. 6 (26 December 1896), 9.

"Studio and Gallery — Cullen, Brymner and Morris discontinue their sketching trip at Beaupré this week." *Saturday Night,* 21 October 1899, p. 9.

"Studio Talk," [on Edmund Morris] *International Studio,* XVII, No. 50 (Apr. 1901), 209 - 210.

[Review of Morris exhibition] *Saturday Night,* 16, No. 17 (7 March 1903), 2.

"Edmund Morris Works. Indian Portraits and Canadian Landscapes at Scott and Son's Gallery." 22 March 1907 (?) [Copy Manitoba Archives, *Edmund Morris Correspondence 1889 - 1913*].

"Fine Drawings of Ojibways. Collection of Artistic and Historic Interest Purchased for the Province." *Telegram.* 20 April 1907.

Boultbee, W. M. "Edmund Morris, Painter." *The Canadian Magazine.* XXXI, No. 2 (May - Oct. 1908), 121 - 127.

"Pictures of Indians." *The Globe.* 18 July 1908.

"Preserving Records of a Passing Race. By Means of Portraits — Mr. Byron E. Walker's Address on Mr. Morris' Portraits of Indians." *Toronto Star.* 20 March 1909.

"Indian Portraits and Curios. Opening of Exhibition Last Night by Mr. Byron E. Walker." *Telegram.* 20 March 1909.

"Fine Paintings by Edmund Morris. Indian Portraits are Highly Praised by Mr. Walker. Vigorous in Drawing. Canada is Behind the United States In Preserving Relics of the Indian Tribes." *The News.* 30 March 1909.

"The Morris Indian Heads." *The News.* 21 April 1909.

The Globe. 8 April 1909.

"A Remarkable Collection of Indian Portraits and Curios." *The Globe.* 10 April 1909.

"Art in Queen's Park, Members Dislike It. Some Criticism of the Purchase of Mr. Morris' Historic Portraits of Indians." [Art Gallery of Ontario, Reference Library. *Canadian Art Club Scrapbooks.]*

"A Painter of Indians." *Saturday Night.* Vol. 22 (24 April 1909) pp. 2 - 3.

"Toronto (Can.)." *American Art News.* New York. 24 April 1909.

"Valuable Indian Portraits." [Banff] *Crag and Crayon.* 10, No. 15, (7 August 1909), 2.

"To Paint Indian Portraits. Edmund Morris Will Visit Brandon Fair to See Sioux Brandon." [Regina] *Morning Leader*. 15 July 1910.

"Toronto artist found drowned. Body of Edmund Morris Discovered on Bank of St. Lawrence. Fell While Sketching. Painter Believed to Have Lost Balance When on Railway Bridge." *The Mail and Empire*. 26 August 1913. [Copy Art Gallery of Ontario, artist's file]

"Edmund Morris Bequeathed Valuable Painting to Public. Distinguished Artist's Will Disposes of Art Treasures. Left Generous Legacies. Celebrated Toronto Painter of Indian Portraits Left Works of Art to the Ontario Museum, Ottawa Collection; British Museum, etc. — Founds Art Scholarship — Reserves Copyright to Family." *Telegram*. 27 Feb. 1914.

"Clever Artist Painted Names in Portraits." By V.I.D., *Sun World*. 6 June 1920.

"A Shame [Prices paid for many Morris paintings very low] *Telegram*. 21 June 1928.

"Edmund Morris (1871 - 1913)." *The Kennedy Quarterly*. IV, No. 1 (Nov. 1963), 40 - 41.

McGill, Jean. "The Indian Portraits of Edmund Morris." *The Beaver*. (Summer 1979), pp. 34 - 41.

_____. "Edmund Morris Among the Saskatchewan Indians and the Fort Qu'Appelle Monument." *Saskatchewan History*. Vol. XXXV, No. 3 (Autumn 1982), 101 - 107.

(c) *Reviews of the period*

"Canadian Art is given fresh stimulus." *World*, 4 February 1908

"The Canadian Art Club, A Review of the Exhibition." by E. F. B. Johnston, *The Mail and Empire*, 8 February 1908

"Canadian Art Club opens Exhibition. First display of organization creates Wide Interest among Lovers of Art." *World*. 9 February [1908].

"The Exhibition of the Canadian Art Club." *Saturday Night*, 22 February 1908.

"An artist of the Habitant." [Profile on H. Walker] *Globe*, 4 May 1908 (?) (Copy AGO, Morris Scrapbooks, "Invoice" book, p. 25)

"Sir William Van Horne on Canadian Art." *Saturday Night*, 5 March 1909.

"Some noted pictures by famous artists at the exhibition of the Canadian Art Club." *The Globe*, 6 March 1909.

["A new estimate of Canada's place in the world of art ..."] *Globe*, 6 March 1909.

"The Canadian Art Club's Second Annual Exhibition." *Saturday Night*, 15 March 1909.

"The Canadian Art Club Amanuensis." *Acta Victoriana*, XXXII, No. 6 (March 1909), 464 - 471.

"A Successful Canadian Sculptor." *Saturday Night,* 8 January 1910.

"Notable Pictures at Art Club's Exhibition." *The Globe,* 16 January 1910.

"The Canadian Art Club exhibition." *Saturday Night,* 22 January 1910.

"Canadian Art. Meritorious Exhibition by Nature Painters opened in the Art Gallery." *Montreal Witness,* 15 February 1910.

"Art Gallery Scene of Fine Exhibit. Many remarkably good paintings and sculptures shown by Canadian artist." *The Montreal Daily Star,* 15 February 1910.

"Visit to the Canadian Art Club's Exhibition in Art Gallery. Canvases are well-displayed and represent High Standard of Canadian Art — Some of the Best described — Four Montrealers are represented." *Montreal Daily Star,* 16 February 1910.

"Famous Canadian Sculptor." [A. P. Proctor] *Winnipeg Telegram,* 16 July 1910.

"Artists honored." *The News,* 9 February 1911.

"Canadian Artists honored." *Saturday Night,* 11 March 1911.

"The Canadian Art Club's exhibition." *Saturday Night,* 11 March 1911.

"An Art Exhibition." *The Canadian Courier,* 11 March 1911, p. 9.

"Lecture by Prof. Mavor. Art and Artists Described at Exhibition." *The Globe,* 17 March 1911.

"Art and artists." *The Globe,* 18 March 1911.

"Notable pictures at the Canadian Art Club's Fourth Annual Exhibition." *The Globe,* 18 March 1911.

"Canadian Art Club. Mr. Ernest Lawson shows Pictures in his Native Country." *Mail,* 27 March 1911.

"The Fine Arts." [Review of Edmund Morris' *Art in Canada: The Early Painters,* Toronto, 1911] *Montreal Daily Star,* 8 April 1911.

"The Canadian Art Club." *Telegram,* 12 February 1912.

"Typical work of Canadian Artists is shown at Fifth Annual Exhibition of the Canadian Art Club." *Weekly Star,* 17 February 1912.

"Canadian Canvases at Art Gallery. Nearly one Hundred in number, and representing Eighteen Exhibitors — Some Comparisons. Mr. Lawson's *Sunlight.* Atkinson's *Return of the Sheep* is a feature picture — Allward's Bell Memorial." *Star,* 17 February 1912.

"Art Club gives fine exhibition. Collection of Pictures representing the work of Eighteen Artists Model for Memorial Striking piece of work by Canadian Sculptor, Walter Allward," *Mail,* 17 February 1912.

"The Annual exhibition of the Canadian Art Club." *Saturday Night* (?) or *Saturday Globe* (?) [1912] (Copy AGO, Morris Scrapbooks, "Invoice" book, p. 105).

Macfall, Haldane. "Art at the Outposts of Empire." *The Academy,* 29 June 1912, pp. 816 - 17.

"At the Canadian Art Club. With two notable canvases at the Club Exhibition." *Canadian Courier.* [Horatio Walker's *Ploughing — First Gleam* and Homer Watson's *The Nut-Gatherers* illustrated] (Copy AGO, Morris Scrapbooks, "Invoice" book, p. 4).

"A Toronto Sculptor's work." [Walter Allward] *Saturday Night* (?). (Copy AGO, Morris Scrapbooks, "Invoice" book, pp. 36 - 37.

Cortissoz, Royal. "The Field of Art." [Article on A. P. Proctor] (Copy AGO, Morris Scrapbooks, "Invoice" book, p. 113).

(d)   *General References: Books, articles and exhibition catalogues*

Allaire, Sylvain. "Les Canadiens au Salon officiel de Paris entre 1870 et 1910: Section Peintre et Dessin." *The Journal of Canadian Art History/Annale D'Histoire de L'Art Canadien,* IV, No. 2 (1977/78), 141 - 151.

Bigsby, John J. *The Shoe and Canoe, or Pictures of Travels in the Canadas.* 2 vols. London: Chapman and Hall, 1850.

Cowan, John Bruce. *John Innes Painter of the Canadian West.* Vancouver: Rose, Cowan & Latta Limited, 1945.

From out of the West ... [Unbound folio of the five Indian portraits by Morris now in the Sask. Gov't Collection: Piapot, Big Darkness, Gambler — Ometaway, Moses, Poundmaker]. Regina: Saskatchewan Department of Industry and Commerce, c. 1975.

Kingston. Agnes Etherington Art Centre, Queen's University, *William Brymner A Retrospective.* 13 May - 1 July 1979. Catalogue by Janet Braide.

——————. *Maurice Cullen 1866 - 1934.* 26 September - 31 October 1982. Catalogue by Sylvia Antoniou.

Lochnan, Katharine A. "The Walker Journals: Reminiscences of John Lavery and William Holman Hunt." *RACAR: Revue d'art canadienne/Canadian Art Review.* IX, Nos. 1 - 2 (1982), 57 - 63.

London. Royal Academy of Arts. *The Hague School, Dutch Masters of the 19th Century,* 1983.

Macdonald, Colin S., comp. "Morris, Edmund Montague," in *Dictionary of Canadian Artists.* Ottawa: Canadian Paperbacks Publishing Limited, 1974. IV, pp. 1297 - 1298.

MacTavish, Newton. *The Fine Arts in Canada.* Toronto: The Macmillan Company of Canada, Limited, 1925.

——————. *Ars Longa.* Toronto: The Ontario Publishing Co., Limited, 1938.

Marius, G. Hermine. *Dutch Painting in the Nineteenth Century.* Trans. Alexander Teixeira de Mattos. London: De La More Press, 1908. Rpt. as *Dutch Painters of the 19th Century,* ed. Geraldine Norman. Suffolk: Baron Publishing, for the Antique Collectors' Club, 1973. Rpt. 1983.

McShine, Kynaston ed. *The Natural Paradise. Painting in America 1800 - 1950.* New York: Museum of Modern Art, 1975. Boston: New York Graphic Society, 1976.

Montreal. Musée des Beaux-Arts. *Images de Charlevoix 1784 - 1950.* 27 November 1981 - 3 January 1982. Catalogue by Victoria A. Baker.

O'Brien, John. "Morrice — O'Conor, Gauguin, Bonnard et Vuillard." *Dossier Art Canadien, Revue de l'Université de Moncton,* 15, Nos. 2/3 (avril - déc. 1982), 9 - 34.

Reid, Dennis. *A Concise History of Canadian Painting.* Toronto: Oxford University Press, 1973.

Saskatoon: Gordon Snelgrove Gallery, University of Saskatchewan, *Grandmaison, Henderson and Kenderdine: Painters of the Prairies.* 14 May - 6 June 1979.

Saskatoon. Mendel Art Gallery, *An exhibition of Paintings by James Henderson 1871 - 1951.* 1969.

Scott, Duncan Campbell. *The Poems of Duncan Campbell Scott.* Toronto: McClelland & Stewart, Publishers, Limited, 1926.

_____. "The Last of the Indian Treaties." *Scribner's Magazine.* 40 (November 1906), pp. 573 - 583.

Slonim, Leon. *A Critical Edition of the Poems of Duncan Campbell Scott.* 2 vols. Ph.D. Diss. University of Toronto, 1978.

Toronto. Art Gallery of Ontario, *Collecting the Hague School in Canada.* 7 May - 26 June 1983. Exhibition organized by Marta Hurdalek.

_____. *Canadians in Paris 1867 - 1914.* 3 March - 15 April 1979. Catalogue by David Wistow.

_____. *Sir Edmund Walker, Print Collector.* 22 November 1974 - 12 January 1975. Catalogue by Katharine A. Jordan [Lochnan].

Toronto: Royal Ontario Museum, *Images of Eighteenth-Century Japan. Ukiyoe Prints from the Sir Edmund Walker Collection.* 1975. Catalogue by David Waterhouse.

Washington. National Collection of Fine Arts, Smithsonian Institution, *American Art in the Barbizon Mood.* 23 January - 30 April 1975. Catalogue by Peter Bermingham.

Windsor. Art Gallery of Windsor, *James Kerr Lawson A Canadian Abroad.* 10 April - 22 May 1983. Catalogue by Robert Lamb.

Winnipeg. Winnipeg Art Gallery, *150 Years of Art in Manitoba.* 1 May - 31 August 1970. Catalogue by Ferdinand Eckhardt.

EDMUND MORRIS : EXHIBITIONS

Exhibitions marked with an asterisk (*) refer to exhibitions mentioned by Morris in his *Diary for 1886 -1904* for which no other documentation has been located. Exhibitions denoted by a dagger (†) are mentioned in reviews of the period and represent only a partial listing of exhibited works. All other exhibition listings have been established from existing catalogues.

1895
* *Art Club* 12 Dec. 1894
    Iroquois
        "painted in Scotland bought by
        D. R. Wilkie, 1896"

        Source: *Diary for 1886 - 1904,* MS.
            pp. 37 and 95

1896
† *Matthews' Gallery, Toronto* 7 March 1896
    watercolours
    View of Notre Dame
    Old Woman Sewing
    Girl Knitting
    Moonlight Scene
    Old Street at Dusk

        Source: Lynne C. Doyle, *Saturday Night*
            9, No. 16 (7 March 1896), 9.

† *Matthews' Gallery, Toronto* 17 October 1896
    Italian Girl
    Moonlight on the Downs, Holland
    Grandmother and Child (watercolour)

        "Painted in Holland, 1896, bought by
        E. F. B. Johnston, 1897"

        Source: *Diary for 1886 - 1904,* MS.
            p. 35
    Muskoka
    St. Andrews, Fifeshire
    Plains of Barbizon
    Nedpath Castle (Peebleshire)

        Source: Lynne C. Doyle, *Saturday Night, 9,*
            No. 49 (24 October 1896), 9

* *Berlin International* (3 May - 30 September)
    1543 Intérieur [Spinning?]

1897
RCA, Ottawa (9 March)
  99 Girl[s] in a Poppy Field
 100 Man in Black
 101 Dutch Interior

OSA, Toronto (13 May)
  58 Girls in a Poppy Field
      (bought by Byron E. E. Walker) $200
  59 The Man in Black 75
  60 Dutch Interior 200
  61 Evening, France 100
 61A Landscape, France 100
 150 Twilight 25
 151 Near the Downs, Holland 20

1898
RCA, Toronto (3 March)
  72 French Canadian Interior
  73 Woman and Child
 198 Children
 199 Interior

1899
RCA, Montreal (7 April)
  86 Landscape, Côte de Beaupré (illus.)
  87 At the Docks low tide
  88 Evening, St. Andrews
  89 The Edge of the Downs, Holland
 190 Evening, Holland
 191 Evening, Ronan
 192 Place du Carrousel, Paris
 193 Street Scene, York, England
 194 Sketch — Dutch Interior

OSA, Toronto (3 March - 23 March)
  40 Landscape
  44 At the Docks, low tide

1900
RCA, Ottawa (15 February)
  78 Landscape, Co. Montmorency
  79 A Habitant Home
 169 St. Féreol Falls, P.Q.
 170 Street Scene, York, England
 171 Landscape, near Alknaar, Holland

OSA, Toronto (3 March - 20 March)
  45 Landscape

Matthews' Gallery, Toronto (17 - 30 November)
Black and White Drawings
39	Chartres	$ 10
40	A Square in Chartres	10
41	In Montmartre, Paris	10
42	At Weston	5
43	Crowfoot, Chief of the Blackfeet Indians	10
44	A Blackfoot Brave	10
45	Big Bear, Chief of the Cree Indians	10

* *Matthews' Gallery, Toronto* (17 - 30 November)
St. Anne's Rapids
"Painted at Beaupré 1898
bought by E. B. Osler 1899. Exhibited
at my one-man exhibition, Toronto,
1900"

Source: *Diary for 1886 - 1904,* MS.
p. 95

Between the Showers
"Painted at Beaupré 1900,
Exhibited one-man exhibition 1900
Toronto, Ont. Academy Toronto 1901.
Bought by F. Nicholls 1900."

Source: *Diary for 1886 - 1904,* MS.
p. 96

October
"Painted at Beaupré 1899
Exhibited at one-man exhibition 1900.
Sold to F. Nicholls afterward
exchanged. Exhibited Manitoba exhibit
1904."

Source: *Diary for 1886 - 1904,* MS.
p. 96

The Harvest Field
"painted 1898
Exhibited Montreal and one-man show
Toronto 1900"

Source: *Diary for 1886 - 1904,* MS.
p. 99

† *Matthews' Gallery, Toronto* (17 - 30 November)
Bathing at Low Tide
A Canadian Landscape
A Landscape
Evening Rapids (loaned by
E. B. Osler, Esq.)
Autumn

Source: "Studio Talk" *International
Studio* XII, No. 50 (April
1901), 209.

1901
RCA, Toronto (12 April)
83   Between the Showers

84   Autumn
85   Poppy Fields (loaned by B. E. Walker, Esq.)

Pan-American Exposition,
Buffalo (1 May - 1 November)
49   Poppy Fields (loaned by B. E. Walker, Esq.)

Glasgow International Exhibition
537   Côte de Beaupré, River St. Lawrence
"painted 1901 from original in
possession of D. R. Wilkie. Exhibited at
the International Exhibition Glasgow
1901, bought by E. R. Wood, Esq.
1902. Exhibited Academy Montreal"

Source: *Diary for 1886 - 1904,* MS.
p. 97

1902
RCA, Montreal (20 March)
117	Côte de Beaupré
118	An Old Mill, France
119	A Harvest Field
120	Spring
221	The Seine, Paris
222	St. Joachim

* *Art Association, Montreal*
A Scotch Valley
"painted 1902. Bought by F. Nicholls,
1903. Exhibited Montreal Art
Association and at Ottawa at the
Academy"

Source: *Diary for 1886 - 1904,* MS.
p. 98

* *Kilmarnock Exhibition, Kilmarnock, Scotland*
A Galloway Landscape
"painted in 1902. Exhibited that year at
the Kilmarnock Exhibit _____ (?)
1904"

Source: *Diary for 1886 - 1904,* MS.
p. 99

1903
RCA, Ottawa (16 April)
86	Scotch Valley (Loaned by Frederick Nicholls, Esq.)
87	Old Scottish Mills
88	Côte de Beaupré, Quebec (Loaned by E. R. Wood, Esq.)
89	Wheat Field
186	St. Joachim, Quebec

Dominion of Canada Industrial Exhibition, Toronto
(27 August - 12 September)
91	Old Scottish Mills	$200
92	Windmills, France	200

93   The Spinner (Loaned by Ontario
      Government)
94   A Poppy Field (Loaned by Byron E.
      Walker, Toronto)

1904
Scott and Sons, Montreal (18 - 31 January)
1   Village and Pine Trees
2   Passing Showers
3   The White Cloud
4   A Laurentian Headland
5   The Grand Battery, Quebec
6   A Fifeshire Village
7   The Fife Coast
8   East Sands, St. Andrews
9   Landscape
10   Willow Trees
11   Abercrombie
12   The Bass Rock
13   Old Mill
14   The Mill Stream
15   The Laurentians
16   Wolfe's Cove, Misty Weather
17   Quebec Landscape
18   Autumn, Côte de Beaupré
19   The Bridge at Beaupré
20   A Galloway Landscape
21   River Scene, Kirkcudbright
22   A Salmon River
23   Evening
24   A Stranded Ship
25   Landscape, Inverary
26   Loch Fyne
27   Landscape
28   Landscape, Fifeshire
29   A Street Scene, York
30   The Dunes, Holland
31   Evening at Sea
32   The Blue Ocean
33   On the Lower St. Lawrence
34   A Village
35   Habitant Houses
36   St. Féreol Falls
37   Willow Trees at Hillhurst
38   In a Valley
39   Evening
40   Landscape
41   At Beauport
42   Cap Diamond, Quebec

Matthews' Art Gallery, Toronto (8 - 22 February)
Source: *Diary for 1886 - 1904,* MS.
p. 91

RCA, Montreal (18 March - 2 April)
113   Cape Tourmente
114   A Quebec Landscape

115   The Coast
116   The Laurentians
117   The Old Fort, Toronto

Universal Exposition, St. Louis,
55   Cape Tourmente
56   A Quebec Landscape
57   The Laurentians

The Arts and Crafts Society of Canada, Toronto
(7 April - 23 April)
157   Decoration for Mantel,
       loaned by Lt.-Col. Pellatt
158   Photograph of Mantelpiece and Decoration

* *Winnipeg, Manitoba*
      October

Source: *Diary for 1886 - 1904,* MS.
p. 96

1905
RCA, Toronto (12 May)
119   Coast Scene, Lower St. Lawrence
120   A Scotch Valley
       (Loaned by F. Nicholls, Esq.)
121   The Grand Battery, Quebec
122   Evening, Cap Tourmente

OSA, Toronto (25 February - 18 March)
75   The Citadel, Quebec $400
76   In the Laurentians   60

J. Wilson & Co., Ottawa (1 - 15 March)
1   Cap Tourmente, River St. Lawrence
2   A Fife Fishing Village
3   The Fife Coast
4   Willow Trees
5   Autumn, Côte de Beaupré
6   Cape Diamond, Quebec
7   The Old Fort, Toronto
8   The Evening, Fifeshire
9   A Windy Morning
10   Willow Trees, Hillhurst
11   The Bridge at Beaupré
12   Evening, the Lower St. Lawrence
13   Old Scottish Mills
14   In the Laurentians
15   The Coast at Beaupré
16   Coast Scene, Lower St. Lawrence
17   Apple Orchard
18   Willow Trees
19   Street Scene, York
20   Place du Carrousel, Paris
21   Landscape, Inverary
22   A Crofter's Home, Argyllshire
23   Loch Fyne

Fig. 39   RCA Exhibition Ottawa, 1906
Visible on far left of upper register is *Cove Fields, Quebec* (cat. 14) first exhibited with
OSA in 1906 as *Old British Earthworks, Quebec.* Morris' *Wolfe's Cove, Quebec* may
be identified above the head of the seated gentleman.
Photo: Public Archives Canada/PA42231

| 84 | Gaspé Sailors | 50 |

RCA, Ottawa (4 May)
126	Old British Earth Works, Quebec "Storm Effect"	
127	Wolfe's Cove, Quebec loaned by D. R. Wilkie, Esq.	
128	A Rancher	
129	Young Sailors Aboard the Snow Queen	
130	Gaspé Sailors	

CNE, Toronto (27 August - 8 September)
140	Evening, Fifeshire	$100
141	A Galloway Landscape	50
142	In Lake Joseph, Muskoka	15
143	Old Scottish Bridge (illus.)	40
144	A Cowboy, Alberta (pastel)	30
145	A Cowboy, Saskatchewan (pastel)	30
146	A Shanty Boy, New Ontario (pastel)	30

1907

OSA, Toronto (23 February - 20 March)
| 89 | The Pic River, Thunder Bay District | $400 |
| 90 | The Very Rev. Dean Houston (Loaned by Stewart Houston, Esq.) | |

RCA, Montreal (1 April)
| 148 | The Pic River, Thunder Bay District | |

1908

CAC, Toronto [Inaugural Exhibition]
(4 - 17 February)
28	A Northern River	
29	The Mourner	
30	Bull Plume (Piegan Chief)	
31	Crowfoot's War Chief	
32	Iron Shield (Blackfoot Head Chief) (loaned by Ontario Government)	
33	Cap Tourmente	
34	Old Scottish Mills	
35	Wolfe's Cove (loaned by D. R. Wilkie)	
36	Bout de l'Isle	
37	Willows	

† *Scott and Son's Toronto* (March ?)
Source: "Edmund Morris Works. Indian Portraits and Canadian Landscapes at Scott and Son's Gallery." 22 March 1907? [Copy Manitoba Archives, *Edmund Morris Correspondence 1889 - 1913*]

RCA, Toronto (24 April)
99	Cap Tourmente	$300
100	The Citadel Quebec	300
101	A Northern River	400

1909

CAC, 2nd Annual, Toronto (1 - 20 March)
42	The Slave	
43	Big Darkness (An Assiniboine) (pastel) [illus.]	
44	A Saulteaux Chief	
45	A Plainsman	
46	A Cree	

CAC, Toronto (29 March - 17 April)
Morris Collection of Indian Portraits at the Gallery of the Canadian Art Club
1	The Wind Blows Fine, Minawasion	
2	Changeable Weather, Quaquagijick	
3	Long Peter, Peter Mitgonabie	
4	Pleasant Time on Earth, Menwekamegemeanang	
5	The Widow Betsy	
6	Through the Sky, Shabagejickwabe	
7	William Odicon	
8	Chief Cheese Quinini	
9	The Man whose Head Touches the Sky, Sakegijickwegabow	
10	Yellow Quill, Auzawaquin	
11	Capetawain	
12	Night Bird, Nepahpenais [illus.]	
13	Man Standing Above Ground, Acoose [illus.]	
14	Sitting White Eagle, Wahpekinewap	
15	Man Sitting in the Middle of the Sun, Nowwekeshequappew	
16	Through the Earth, Shabokamik	
17	Water, Ochopowace	
18	Splashing Water, Chakikum	
19	Spring Man, Kahmeeusekahmaweyencw [illus.]	
20	The Man who Ties the Knot, Kakapechamaskis	
21	Feather, Mequinis [illus.]	
22	Pimotat	
23	The Front Man, Nikanabeao	
24	Bear's Hat, Kyaiyistumokon	
25	The Cutter Woman, Sisoyake	
26	Chief Weasel Calf, Apaunista	
27	John Three Bulls, Called Drunken Chief	
28	A Far Away Voice, Piiskini	
29	Slow Coming Over the Hill, Itspecotamisow	
30	Head Chief Iron Shield, Ixkimauotani [illus.]	
31	Chief Crow Shoe, Mastoitsikin	
32	Calf Child, War Chief of the Blackfeet, Unistaipoka	
33	Head Chief Running Rabbit, Atsistaumukkon	
34	Head Chief Yellow Horse, Otokumiotas	
35	Black Eagle, Sixsipita	
36	Chief Bull Plume, Stumiksisapo [illus.]	
37	Man Angry with Hunger, Minnikonotsi	
38	Eagle Flying Against the Wind,	

Pitamowinasi
39   Chief Running Wolf, Apisomakau [illus.]
40   Head Chief Butcher, Stokinota
41   Chief Big Swan, Akamakai
42   Chief Bull Shield, Stumixowotan
43   Chief Strangle Wolf, Maquaestupistn
44   Chief Blackfoot, Old Woman, Apinocomita
45   Joe Healy, Potina [illus.]
46   Mike Oka
47   Too Cloudy
48   Fish Carrier
49   Antoine Hoke, Medicine Man [illus.]
50   Chief Carry the Kettle, Chagakin
51   Big Darkness, Opazatonka [illus.]
52   Chief Peter Wesley of the Stonies
53   Dan Wildman
54   Head Chief Little Chief, Tcillah [illus.]
55   Chief Big Wolf

RCA, Art Gallery and Public Library, Hamilton
(25 November)
100   Cove Fields, Quebec
101   Evening, Beaupré
102   The Citadel, Quebec
103   Landscape, Beauport, Quebec

1910
CAC, 3rd Annual, Toronto (7 - 27 January)
47   Coming Storm (Alberta) [illus.]
48   The Foothills (A Scout)
49   The Porcupine Hills (Ancient Buffalo Corral)
50   Wolf Collar (A Medicine Man)
     (pastel) [illus.]
51   Spring Chief of the Blackfeet
52   Little Shield of the Blackfeet
53   Water Chief of the Blackfeet

CAC, Montreal (14 February - 12 March)
44   Coming Storm, Alberta [illus.]
45   In the Foothills — A Scout
46   Head Chief Iron Shield of the Blackfeet
     [illus.]
47   Chief Bull Plume of the Piegans
48   Big Darkness, An Assiniboine
49   Meguinis, A Cree (lent by the Ontario
     Government)
50   The Cove Fields, Quebec

CNE, Toronto (27 August - 12 September)
138   Wolfe's Cove, Quebec (lent by
      D. R. Wilkie, Esq., Toronto) $200
139   Cove Fields, Old British Earth Works,
      Quebec [illus.]   700
140   Man angry with hunger,
      old Piegan Indian   200
141   Little Shield, Blackfoot Indian   200
RCA, Montreal (24 November)
143   An Old Cree Indian
144   A Saulteaux — Thunder Bay

1911
CAC, 4th Annual, Toronto (3 - 25 March)
37   Landscape, Old Fort Edmonton
38   The Plains of Alberta (Blackfoot Lodges)
39   An Ojibway Encampment (Thunder Bay
     District)
40   Chief Nepahpenais of the Saulteaux
     (lent by the Saskatchewan Government)
41   A Saulteaux Brave (lent by the Saskatchewan
     Government) [illus.]
42   Landscape
43   Blackfoot Lodges
44   Chateaux Frontenac, Quebec [illus.]
45   The Dufferin Terrace, Quebec

RCA, Toronto (23 November)
124   A Faraway Voice — Blackfoot Indian
      (Pastel)
125   Chief of the Bloods (Pastel)
126   A Blood Indian (Pastel) (Lent by the Ontario
      Government)

1912
CAC, 5th Annual, Toronto (8 - 27 February)
52   A Saskatchewan Landscape, Evening [illus.]
53   Coming Storm — The Country of the Crees
54   Encampment of Chief Star Blanket
55   Cree Lodges
56   Evening in the File Hills [illus.]
57   Northern Lights
58   Toronto Bay
59   Night at Hanlan's Point
60   An Idyll
61   The Citadel (Quebec)
62   Evening (The Citadel)
63   Dunes of Holland (Lent by
     Sir Edmund Walker)

RCA, Ottawa (28 November)
169   Saskatchewan Landscape
170   St. Monance, Fifeshire
171   Cap Tourmente, Quebec
172   Railway Camp, Northern Ontario (Pastel)
173   Galicians on Strike, Railway Camp (Pastel)

RCA, Winnipeg (16 December)
114   The Cove Fields, Quebec
115   Cree Lodges in the File Hills
116   Little Shield, a Blackfoot Indian

1913
CAC, 6th Annual, Toronto (9 - 31 May)
65   In the Country of the Crees — Sask.
     (4 decorated skin lodges) [illus.]
66   In the Foot Hills (Assiniboine Lodges)
67   Evening, In the Foot Hills
68   Landscape — Saskatchewan
69   Nepahpenais (Chief of the Saulteaux)
70   A Cree

114

Fig. 40 Installation Canadian Art Club, 6th
Annual, 9 - 31 May 1913, Public Reference Library
Gallery, St. George & College Sts., Toronto.
At right: Edmund Morris, *In the Foot Hills
(Assiniboine Lodges)* no. 66
Photo: Art Gallery of Ontario, Toronto

Fig. 41 Installation CAC, 6th Annual, 9 - 31 May
1913
Centre: Edmund Morris, *In the Country of the
Cree — Sask.* (no. 65)
Photo: Art Gallery of Ontario, Toronto

71 The Coast of Ile d'Orelans, Quebec
72 Landscape (Inverary, Argyllshire)
73 Neidpath Castle

CNE, Toronto (23 August - 8 September)
324 A Saskatchewan Landscape $700

1914
CAC, 7th Annual (1 - 30 May)
31 Cape Diamond from the St. Lawrence
   (Lent by D. R. Wilkie) [illus.]
32 The Cornfield, Ste Anne de Beaupré, Quebec
   (Lent by D. R. Wilkie) [illus.]
33 The Coast of Ile d'Orleans, Quebec
   (Lent by Miss Morris)
34 Buffalo Willows
35 Cove Fields (Quebec)
36 Willows (Haddingtonshire, Scotland)
37 Cap Tourmente, Ile d'Orleans
   (Lent by Wm. Morris)
38 A Cree

1922
The Art Gallery of Toronto (11 February - 12 March)
133 Spinning (1895) Lent by the Ontario
   Government
   [destroyed by fire in the 1950s]
134 Windy Morning (1898), Lent by
   Major A. B. Wilkie

1928
OSA, Toronto (3 March - 8 April)
Edmund Morris Memorial Exhibition Art Gallery of Toronto
1 Ten Portraits of Indian Chiefs (Lent by the
   Royal Ontario Museum)
2 Chief Bull Plume (Property of the
   Art Gallery of Toronto)
3 The Poppy Field (Property of the Art Gallery
   of Toronto)
4 Indian Chief (Lent by Alexander
   C. Morris, Esq.)
5 Pastel Landscape (Lent by Alexander
   C. Morris, Esq.)
6 Water Colour Figure Study
   (Lent by Alexander C. Morris, Esq.)
7 Girl Knitting (Lent by Alexander
   C. Morris, Esq.)
8 Windy Morning, Quebec (Lent by
   Major Wilkie)
9 Wolfe's Cove, Quebec (Lent by
   Major Wilkie)
10 Quebec (Lent by Mrs. W. A. H. Kerr)
11 Indian Encampment
12 The Slave

13 The Saint Lawrence Near Quebec
14 Dufferin Terrace, Quebec
15 Indian Encampment on the Prairie
16 Western Indian Encampment
17 Twilight
18 Windmills
19 Woodland Pasture
20 The Edge of the Downs, Holland
21 French-Canadian Farms
22 Low Tide
23 Western Cowboy
24 Moonlight
25 Head Study
26 Passing Showers
27 Cree Lodges
28 Cap Tourmente from Island of Orleans
29 The Coast of Beaupré
30 Indian Village
31 Castle on the Hill
32 Landscape, Inverary
33 Quebec Farm
34 Autumn
35 Fishing Boat, Low Tide
36 Coast Scene
37 Pasture Land
38 Autumn Evening
39 Rocky Coast
40 A Spaniard
41 Silver and Gray
42 The Mill Stream
43 Golden Harvest
44 French-Canadian House
45 Coming Storm
46 In Camp
47 Dufferin Terrace
48 Cape Diamond
49 The Artist
50 Fisherman
51 Low Tide, June
52 The Ramparts, Quebec
53 Lower Town, Quebec
54 Pioneer Days
55 The Village
56 The Procession
57 Story Telling
58 Hill and Valley
59 The Red Barn
60 The Pool
61 The Prairie
62 Woodland
63 Winding Road
64 Evening, Lower Town, Quebec
65 Rising Moon
66 The Landing Place
67 A Crofter's Home

1935

The Art Gallery of Toronto, (November)
136   Chief Bull Plume

1939

CNE, Toronto (22 August - 6 September)
148   Head of Chief Blackfoot, Iron Shield
         (Lent by the National Gallery of Canada)

1952

CNE, Toronto (22 August - 6 September)
 80   Chief Bull Plume, Stumisksisapo Piegan

1962

Museum of the Plains Indians, Browning, Montana
         Algonkian and Siouan Indians of the
         Far West
         An Art Exhibition from the Collection of the
         Glenbow Foundation in Calgary
         Bad Boy (Glenbow Museum)
         Moonias (Glenbow Museum)
         Nepahpenais (Night Bird) (Glenbow
         Museum)
         Opazatonka (Big Darkness) (Glenbow
         Museum)
         Peter Mitgonabie (Long Peter) (Glenbow
         Museum)

1970

Winnipeg Art Gallery, Winnipeg (1 May - 31 August)
150 Years of Art in Manitoba
140   Indian Encampment on Prairie (Art Gallery
         of Ontario)
141   Chief Yellow Quill (ROM) [illus.]
142   Maskegon or Swampy — Capetawa,
         Yellow Quill (ROM)

APPENDIX B

Edmund M. Morris A.R.C.A. by G. A. Reid, Toronto 17 March 1924
Toronto: Art Gallery of Ontario, Archives (typescript)

The career of Edmund M. Morris, A.R.C.A., was short but was crowded with varied activity and high accomplishment. Coming from a prominent Canadian family, he had that pride of family which made him treasure its records, and the fact that his Father, Alexander Morris, was at one time Lieutenant-Governor of Manitoba, bringing him into close touch with the Indian tribes of the west, gave the artist Morris an impetus which resulted in his great series of Indian portraits now in the Royal Ontario Museum and other places. Those influences may also have contributed to the marked strain of patriotism which was shown in many different ways, not only during his life, but in the remarkable will left at his death by which the varied character of his activities became known. This will is published here, not only because it is an explanation of the reason for this exhibition and sale of his paintings, but because it provides such a vivid picture of his character, and sets forth the many activities of his short life.

Edmund Montague Morris was born in Perth, Ontario in 1871, and at the age of 42 was drowned in the St. Lawrence River near Quebec where he was sketching. He began his studies as an artist under William Cruikshank in Toronto, and continued his studies first at the Art Student's League, New York, and afterwards in Paris in the Julian Academy. On his return to Canada he painted a number of figure pictures, but later became interested in Canadian Landscape, working in a vigorous modern style. He kept up his figure work to some extent and his latest work was the remarkable series of Indian portraits, which it was possible only to have done through the great friendship of his Father with the Indians.

Mr. Morris was largely instrumental in organizing the Canadian Art Club, which held together for about ten years. This was a group of Canadian painters who seceded to some extent from the main art body of Ontario, and who through the strong management of Mr. Morris as its secretary, made a number of excellent Exhibitions. Mr. Morris was an Associate member of the Royal Canadian Academy, and is represented by paintings in the National Gallery, the Toronto Art Gallery, the Royal Ontario Art Museum and other public collections.

Portion of the Will of the Late Edmund M. Morris, A.R.C.A.

Relating to Public Bequests.

"Regarding my pictures," states the will, "a selection is to be made and sold by auction or by private sale, the proceeds to go as a scholarship in the Ontario College of Art. To the art museum of Toronto I leave my books of art, my etchings and Japanese prints, and to the Royal Victoria Museum my engravings. To the Royal Ontario Museum I leave the black walnut cabinet given to my grandfather by Dr. Wilson, one of the fathers of geology in Canada, the four old colonial book cases, two of which are from the old military settlement on the Rideau.

"The other two, made of the doors of old Beverley House (homestead of the Beverley Robinson family, at the corner of Queen and John streets, torn down to make room for the Methodist Book Room), the round table, the set of habitant chairs, grandfather's arm chairs, Dutch clock, delft and such other articles as the committee think would illustrate the colonial days in Canada, these to be grouped together in some section of the museum. It is advisable that something should appear to remind us of old colonial days.

"To the Royal Victoria Museum, Ottawa, I bequeath my negatives and photographs, which I made during the time spent with the native tribes, enlargements of certain of these to be made and hung together as a collection, and it is my wish if I am unable to complete my account of the tribes that this work be edited, and if it is deemed advisable, published.

"My valuable collection of Indian relics I will to the Royal Ontario Museum, it to be kept intact, as a collection and called the Morris collection and placed in the same gallery and contiguous with my Indian portraits, which are the property of the Ontario Government.

"The copyright of these portraits which I own reverts to my family and might by them be sold to the Government.

"I desire to have a selection made of my Indian negatives, enlargements made and a set presented to the British Museum, the Winnipeg Museum and the Montreal Art Association, also the Dick Institute, Kilmarnock, and also the Museum of Colmer Alsace, and regarding the Indian portraits still in my possession, the one called the Iron Shield to the National Gallery, Ottawa, and the others, one to the Art Gallery, Toronto, the Winnipeg Art Gallery, the Montreal Art Association, one to the town of Morrisburgh, Glen Morris and Morris, Man.

"My books on Canada and the Revolutionary period in America to the Morris section of Queen's College Library, my books on the Indians to the Royal Ontario Museum or rather to the Ethnological and Archaelogical Department of the Government of Ontario.

"My books to be given to the Arts and Letters Club, Toronto.

"The Morris manuscripts I will to the Archives Department, Ottawa. These are laid in volumes and include the correspondence of Hon. William Morris, the Hon. Alexander Morris and mine own regarding the native tribes of Canada and art."

PHOTOGRAPHY CREDITS

Art Gallery of Hamilton, cat. 13; Art Gallery of Ontario, figs. 10, 20, 21, 40, 41, 42, cats. 1, 19, 36; Glenbow Museum, cat. 15; The Government of Alberta, figs. 8, 27, 29, 31, cats. 21, 22, 23, 24, 25; the Government of Ontario, fig. 14, cats. 16, 17; The Government of Saskatchewan, figs. 25, 34, cats. 27, 28, 29, 30, 31, 32, 33, 34; Manitoba Archives, Winnipeg, frontispiece, figs. 1, 7, 16, 22, 23, 24, 26, 28, 30, 32, 35, cat. 37; Metropolitan Toronto Library, fig. 12, cat. 6; Musée du Québec, figs. 3; National Gallery of Canada, figs. 4, 11, 13, cats. 12, 14; Norman Mackenzie Art Gallery, Don Hall, figs. 5, 33, cats. 7, 8, 9, 10, 18, 20, 26, 35, 38, 39; Ontario Archives, Toronto, fig. 17; Public Archives of Canada, figs. 6, 39; Queen's University Archives, Kingston, figs. 18, 19; Reading Public Museum and Art Gallery, fig. 15; Royal Ontario Museum, Canadiana Collection, cats. 2, 4, 5; Women's Canadian Historical Society, Toronto, cat. 3; M. O. Hammond (courtesy Art Gallery of Ontario), p. 63.